CONQUERING DRAMA

I0197225

By Maha Vajra

This book is the transcription and summary editing of various seminars given by Master MahaVajra. They are arranged in a way to coherently fit together It is to be read as if you are present at a seminar.

F.Lepine Publishing

Copyright 2011
ISBN: 978-1-926659-10-7

www.MahaVajra.com

Table of Contents

Part 1

Truth is Not the Words we Use

For some people, conquering drama and attaining immovable happiness (often referred to as *enlightenment* by many) means paying a certain amount to a specific organization, sect, or guru. For some others, enlightenment is attained by consuming funny hallucinogenic products. For others, enlightenment is found by reading every book they can get their hands on, listening to every audio track they can find, and attending as many seminars as humanly possible. Yet, for others, enlightenment is cutting yourself away from the world, so that you can live a hermit life. All that said, if enlightenment exists, there must be someone who is right. Someone somewhere must have experienced it. Someone must know the truth!

Some people will tell you that I am enlightened. Don't trust them. They can't know this for sure. Well, maybe some rare people can, but most can't. What's more, I can't prove to you that I am either. However, whether I am enlightened or not is irrelevant anyway. Why? Because truth is not an information. It's an experience. What matters is what you get out of the experiences that you have.

I'll give you an example to illustrate my point. Let's say you travel out to a desert in Africa and go to some village to explain to the locals what snow is.

"Hey people, listen up: I'm going to teach you something you don't know today. I'll talk to you about *snow*! Snow is like white cotton falling from the sky. It's cold and when it touches you, it becomes water."

After hearing you say all of that, they'll probably look at each other with a puzzled look on their face and wonder if you've smoked those aforementioned funny things that make someone *enlightened*. They may laugh at you, ignore you, they may burn you on a pillar to "save your soul", they may ask you for food or medicine, or they may listen to you with a genuine interest to discover more. But, one thing is for sure: they most certainly will not have a true understanding of what snow is aside from the sterile words and examples you used in your best effort to make them experience it.

Even if the words you use make sense, even if the individual concepts you use are common knowledge for those people, they will never grasp the complete truth of what you are trying to convey no matter how clever your examples and explanations may be.

Now, bring those villagers in a place where there is snow. Let them touch it, taste it, smell it. Let them play with it, let them have a snowball fight, build igloos, slide on it, etc. Only then will they truly grasp what snow is. "Ah!! Snow! So this is what snow is! Hey, you're right: snow is like white cotton falling from the sky. It's cold, and when it touches you it turns to water!" Now all the examples and words make total sense for them.

The same thing would apply if you had never tasted a chocolate cake. I could spend months telling you about flour, cocoa, eggs and milk. I could explain to you what the texture of the cake is like, how it melts in your mouth, how it smells. I could get you to speak with the baker who invented the recipe, or the guy who built the oven that cooked the cake. None of this will ever, ever make you experience the truth of what a chocolate cake is. To find out, you must experience it for yourself.

Since I have no other tools than words to convey the experience of a chocolate cake to you, all I can do is use those words and examples hoping that somehow I will pull enough strings in you to make you "get it".

So, we use words to refer to experiences, and *enlightenment* is such a word. But, have you experienced it? If not, regardless of how much effort I would put into explaining it, at best you will have some vague concept of what enlightenment is. You'll only really get it when you get there.

Thus, nothing proves to you that I am englightened, and most of you are not enlightened, so don't trust me. Actually, don't fear me, either. The only thing you can do is to trust your own experience. Your experience *is* the truth. Trust it. Trust yourself. Trust what you feel. Trust what you experience. Upon reading this book, you'll be triggered through different states of being. This is where truth lies. The words and examples I'll use in the coming pages are merely pointing to it.

If you feel that this book is not for you, you are blessed with something called free will. Nobody forces you to read it. No one has power over your mind (not even an enlightened person). So, if you don't like the experience you have while reading it, respect yourself and put it down. On the otherhand, if you do like what you experience along the way, then respect yourself also and keep reading, experimenting, and integrating. Don't take my word for it. I can't prove what enlightenment is to you. All we can do together is to experience stuff, so, we'll play along. In live seminars, and to a lesser degree, in live online events, I have other tools to communicate like non-verbal cues, tone of voice, etc. I play mind tricks and word games with attendees, I laugh, act, and talk stupid. It's all okay. Here in writing, I don't have the luxury of using non-verbal cues, so I'll do my best to trigger experiences through written words alone.

Ready? Let's play :)

We're Screwed!

Please close your eyes and breathe deeply. Bring your focus inwards, within you. Imagine that every cell of your body is a happy, smiling face. Imagine every part of you is smiling, from the tiniest particle all the way up to your entire body, and even beyond. Keep on breathing slowly, and focus on happiness. Imagine evey single of one your neurons is a happy face sending laughing signals through your nervous system. Imagine your brain as being light and merry. Keep breathing deeply, and rejoice at the discovery that every air molecule entering your lungs is a happy face bringing nourishment to your happy faced cells...shuttling through what seems to be giant water slides...being your circulatory system.

You can smile, or giggle, or even laugh if you feel like (but don't force it). Saturate yourself with this experience of happiness and stay there. Just feel it, and breathe deeply. Stay there. Stay happy, happy, happy... You feel completely overwhelmed by this *happy* state.

*Note: It is important to do this technique at least once to grasp the full extent of everything that is contained in this book (as you will see in the coming chapters).

After having done this for a couple of minutes, slowly come back to your regular conscious state. Please pay close attention, because if you wish to conquer drama in your life, this teaching is at the very core of the majority of the techniques I teach. It is the foundation on which everything else will be built. I will often talk to you about *experience* throughout this book. What you just had is exactly that: an experience. You most likely felt the happiness. You had that feeling of being happy. But, let me ask you this: Did you have a good reason to feel this happiness? No, you didn't. Of course, you read words that suggested it, and there was an external influence to trigger this in you, but you could do it anytime now without me ever writing or saying anything to you, could you not?

You felt happiness simply because you focused on it.

True happiness is the one that you experience when you have no reason to be happy. If you feel bliss because of your wonderful wife, husband or kids, eventually this or those people will die or go away. If you're happy because you have this wonderful job, some day you'll lose it, or you'll retire, or get fired. Something will happen. It will end. So, please don't make the mistake of believing that your job, your car, your house, your spouse, or whatever else out there is a solid reason for you to be truly happy. We just experienced happiness for no reason; and we also know that nothing out there lasts forever.

But of course it's fun to have people we love around, and a good job, and things to own, but the only happiness that remains unaffected by the gain or the loss of any of this is the one that you feel for absolutely no reason, save for your own will to feel it. Period. You felt a certain feeling of happiness just a couple of minutes ago when you contemplated happy faces in your body. You had no reason to, but you felt it just because you focused your mind on it.

Remember I said earlier I like to use mind tricks and games as teaching tools? Well, I just tricked you. You felt happy just because you put your attention on happiness. But, hear this (even if you may not like it): Some of the suffering you have in your life also arises because you want it and because you put your focus on it. I proved it to you using imaginary happy faces. The same method works for sad ones.

There are things that pull us out of this state of happiness. We concentrate on wanting a wonderful life, and something happens and pulls us out of our natural state of happiness. Sometimes, it even pushes us into a state of suffering.

What's going on?

Well, I have news for you: We're screwed!

We'll have to be happy and we'll have to suffer. That's life. You can buy this car, wear those clothes, have that kind of physical appearance, listen to this music, own that home, take that "blue pill" or whatever else. There will always be someone somewhere trying to convince you that if you buy or get *this* thing, you'll be happy. Some others will try to prove to you that you can stay happy and avoid all suffering if you have the correct mindset.

However, no matter how you look at it, there has never, ever been a single human being, even the most saintly ones (especially the most saintly ones) who attained immovable happiness without experiencing suffering. It's part of life. Oh, of course you can learn to be comfortable in your suffering, but suffering you will experience. That's unavoidable.

However, you can also learn to be comfortable in your happiness, that's much better. All in all, there is an equivalent amount of happiness and of suffering in life. Except for the extra bonus happiness, which is the kind of happiness that you feel for no reason.

The bliss you feel when people you love come close to you will be equivalent to the suffering you feel when they go away. Through deaths, conflicts, breakups, sickness, problems, evolving mindsets, shifting outlooks on life, etc. It doesn't matter. Everything that is outside of you carries it's charge of happiness and suffering. That's life. Again, there is only one exception: the happiness you experience for no reason other than you simply wanting it. However, a good mindset will not prevent the flow of life and natural forces from affecting you. So, there will be good moments and bad moments. This is normal.

Some people refer to me as a Buddhist, since I often talk about the wisdom of the Buddha. So, just to throw them a curveball now and then, I talk to them about other great teachings and teachers. Those who think I'm a Buddhist often hear me tell this story about two girls who came to Jesus asking him: "You have to come and heal Lazarus, because he's going to die!"

What we usually learn in traditional Christian teachings is to ask what we want, with faith, and we'll get it. So the story goes that Jesus went to Lazarus, raised his hand and Lazarus was resurected. But that's not the story. There's a little known part of that story, the most important part in fact, that not many people put emphasis on.

When the two girls, who were the sisters of Lazarus, came to Jesus to ask him to come and heal the poor guy as he was about to die, not only did Jesus not rush to the scene immediatly, but he even turned his back on the two girls and said, "Why do you think this suffering is in vain? Don't you know my father has a plan?" That is the teaching of Jesus: Suffering has a purpose. It brings wisdom. No suffering, no wisdom. No happiness, no wisdom either. You need the range of experiences to get wisdom and to know how to handle yourself and stay in balance in life.

Here's an example to illustrate my point: Put a young child on a bike when he's old enough to ride on his own, and explain to him or her all the intellectual reasons behind the importance of staying in balance on the bike. The first thing the kid will do is hop on the bike, pedal a bit, crash and get hurt. It's not because he or she didn't undestand what you said, but there was no experience conveyed through your explanations. Only empty words.

Once the child experiences the suffering of falling, that's it: wisdom has come. From then on, you could try to convince the kid to crash and fall on the ground on purpose. You could hire lawyers to build a case vouching for the benefits of falling down. But, nothing will do: The kid will still do everything he or she can to stay in balance. Why? Because there was suffering.

That means that everything you did in your life in your best effort to explain to kids how to avoid suffering was almost all useless. The only thing grown ups can do is to guide kids through the suffering and the happiness so that they will gain wisdom. So, a directive, sterile, "Don't do that!" won't work. They need to experience the happiness and joy of riding in balance and the suffering and pain of falling on the ground to gain wisdom and to truly grasp why and how to stay in balance on the bike (or in life). That's how it works.

Are you starting to compare what I'm saying here with your own life experience thinking: "Yeah, I did haphazardly try to stay in balance in a few situations, and I hurt myself. Now, because of that, I did everything to stay in balance from that point on "?

It is through your own life experiences that you find happiness. When we were very young, we were unknowingly very happy. Of course, we didn't have as many responsibilities; but that's not the point I'm trying to make. What I mean is that we were happy, but we didn't know that we were because we hadn't really suffered yet.

How do you know that light exists? You've never seen it. Oh, you see what light reflects upon: the floor, the walls, the trees, and everything else you see. But, you don't see light itself. Still, you know that light exists, because if we put the light out, you experience darkness. Through darkness you deduce that there is light; and through suffering you deduce that there is happiness.

I'm trying to find ways to get you to think about it: What is life made of? Why am I here? What is going on? I can't tell you the truth, because the truth is an experience and not a fact nor an information. What I can do is chit-chat with you and hope that it will summon an experience that will make you feel something through experience.

We will do another technique that is just as important as the happy facing technique we did a bit earlier. Now, this technique is taking it a step further; you will tackle painful emotions head on: I would like you to pick a moment in your life when you felt abandonment or rejection. Don't pick a very intense moment, but it has to be challenging enough to make you uncomfortable. Take the time to do it. Just summon back the emotion, without trying to resolve it, nor forgive it, nor free yourself from it. Don't try to change it. Just become aware of the experience of abandonment or of rejection. Pull it up, let it come out, feel it. Just sit there. Just look, feel, and breathe...

What we are doing now is a controlled observation of a moment of suffering. Sit still in it. Again, don't try to interact with it, influence it, or resolve it. Don't embellish it, nor dramatize it. Simply discover how the more you observe it, the more it is losing its power over you: simply because you are paying attention to it. Notice that what was disturbing you at first is now merely information. Not comfortable information I agree, but information nonetheless. You paid attention, you took deep breaths, you observed it, you relaxed into it despite the initial discomfort, and now it has lost its power over you.

One word of advice: When you are done doing this technique, don't just get up and remain with that aftertaste of suffering in your mouth. First, pay attention to the pain of abandonment or rejection. And, when you have observed it long enough so that it has lost its grip on you, fill yourself with happy faces. Remember the happy facing trick we did earlier? Do exactly that. While still breathing deep and looking inwards, replace the bad feeling of the painful experience you brought back to the surface with happy faces...imagining every single cell of your body as a happy face: your bloodstream, your nervous system, the food you're digesting, your organs, etc. Every, and all of those things, are happy faces! You can even smile if it helps create the right experience!

By paying attention to an experience of suffering, it naturally recedes. You don't resolve it just yet, but you accept it and in doing so it loses it's power over you. This new, more positive and more fertile mindset will have a huge affect on you and on the way you observe things and manage events in your life.

When I teach this technique in seminars, I can monitor people doing it and it never fails: everybody is amazed at how it is true that the sting of the pain is not as painful anymore. Some even break into laughter, still teary-eyed from remembering a painful event, feeling for the first time that they don't have to be the victim of their painful emotions anymore. It is quite a liberating experience! "It's so easy!", they say, after having done it even only once!

But if it's so easy, why don't we all instinctively do it? Why don't we pay attention to our painful emotions if this is all it takes to make them much less painful? Well, the reasons why we don't naturally do it stem from an instinct of survival. We were made that way. We were made to deny. So, if you are in denial and refusing to look at what hurts you within yourself, don't feel bad. You're doing exactly what you've been programmed to do. What I am proposing is a way to override that built-in program.

Let's talk about it...

The Dungeon: Blocks and Chains

In the preceding image, we have a human being and we have what we'll call *an experience of happiness,* as well as *an experience of un-happiness.* This is kindergarten level wisdom, but please bear with me.

So, I just asked you to re-awaken an experience when you felt abandonmnent or rejection, just as it was, without dramatizing it. Simply breathing into the uncomfortable feeling and emotion.

Unknowingly, we usually keep these emotions inside us. Over time, they condense in some sort of figurative concrete and create what we will call *blocks*. These blocks end up being unconsciously piled-up between us and the experience of happiness. At the same time, we also create what we could refer to as *chains*. Those chains tie us down to numerous anchor points within us. All this has been solidified over the years. So much so, that until we discover how to use this emotional construction (or destruction) kit, we are somewhat prisoner of this dungeon, of this inner fortress.

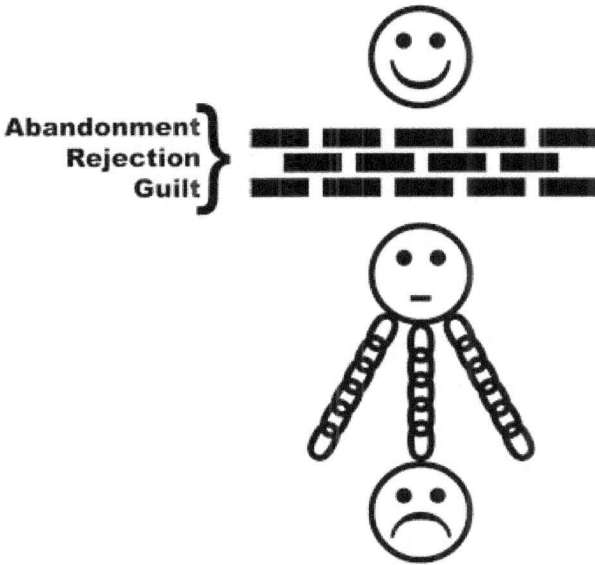

Abandonment
Rejection
Guilt

So, there is a dungeon, within the confines of which we are chained down to stuff (which causes suffering) surrounded by walls that block out happiness, making it inaccessible for us. That seems like a pretty bad place to be, doesn't it!? But, what exactly are those building blocks that pile-up and build-up that dungeon which traps us? Humans have three broad types of emotional clogs that serve as raw materials to make up those blocks we've been talking about. We'll call those raw materials Abandonment, Rejection, and Guilt.

Those are the three emotions that congeal into hard blocks and pile-up, effectively building emotional walls into a fortress around us. This kind of leaves us in a pretty harsh and inhospitable ground to grow and be happy, doesn't it? But those walls can very simply be torn down. How? In exactly the same way as we just did a few pages ago: by sitting down and gazing at them. Consciousness is the solvent that will "melt" the concrete and break apart the walls of that fortress.

What we actually do when we refuse to look at our experiences of suffering is ask our soul to project them in our life in a more intense manner, so that eventually we have no choice but to go through those emotions and look at them consciously. This is when what we perceive as being *bad stuff* happens.

If you take the time to contemplate emotions before they are dense enough to manifest in your physical reality, they just won't. Taking the time to dissolve the emotional blocks before they create events in your life, will prevent a lot of "bad stuff" to happen to you. After that, you will have only blessings. This is how we manifest, this is how we create. Actually, doing this little trick of conscious observation will not allow you to create good events: you'll just stop creating the painful ones.

But how can you, the reader, do that? How can you dissovle painful emotions and stop manifesting painful events in your life? One block, one emotion at a time! And to do this, the first place to begin is as I have already mentioned: just sit in the painful emotion and observe it consciously, without interacting with it nor believing in the drama that your mind will try to throw at you.

However, as you may guess, that's not all there is to the story. You also need to know why the blocks are still there in order to completely dissolve them. Otherwise, if the underlying reasons that created the blocks in the beginning are still in place, the blocks will soon build back up.

Like I said, we don't only have walls blocking out the happiness; we also have chains that attach us to mundane things. We will call them, quite obviously, attachments

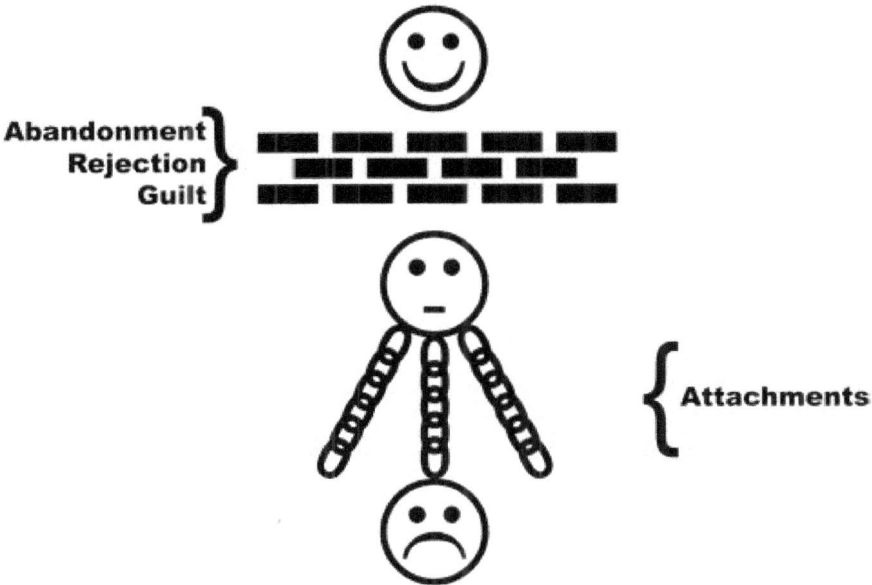

We are attached to our spouse, our kids, our sisters and brothers, our jobs, our car, our house, our this and our that. To free ourselves from all this, we must strive to experience what we will call non-attachement. But beware in your interpretation of the words! *Non-attachment* does not mean *getting rid of.* It doesn't mean not to enjoy the things you own, and it certainly doesn't mean to stop loving and caring for those you love.

You still have things that you can appreciate. You can still have relationships with people. You can still have a good paying job to support you within this world. This is all good. It's all blessing. However, the true essence of non-attachment allows someone to just let go when impermanence comes around and when stuff or people have to go. Non-attachment simply means not to hold on when the inevitable happens, as it is this holding on that is painful. Everytime you hold on, the pull on the chains hurt. The stronger the chain, the more intense the pain.

In a nutshell, this is basically how we fight with life. We deploy considerable amounts of effort that are, despite our best intentions, illusory, trying to prevent the divine flow of life. This is not only pointless, but it is also painful. Like we saw earlier, the pain is what allows us to learn how to stay in balance. However, if suffering is inevitable, you can certainly learn to process it more efficiently. Many are looking for that *magic* pill or method, and many are willing to sell it to you.

You can buy hundreds of New Age books that will essentially tell you: "You can be happy just by having the correct mindset, by doing this mantra, by taking this pill, by smoking this herb... This is how you will find enlightenment and everlasting bliss!" It's true that there are many paths to enlightenment. The Buddha himself said that there are thousands of them (but I doubt he was referring to pills and wishful thinking).

But before going any further, we should try to find a good definition of what enlightenment is if we are going to keep talking about it. How about we use the definition of the Buddha himself? After all, he's not that incompetent about this issue, wouldn't you agree?

His definition is as follows: Enlightenment is not suffering. Simple, and easy.

So, he doesn't say what enlightenment *is* but rather what it is *not*. When there is nothing in you supporting suffering, you're enlightened, which is why we often refer to enlightenment as constant happiness. That being said, you don't really *attain* enlightenment. Rather, you stop attaining non-enlightenment. You just stop supporting what is not enlightening you by looking at everything that makes you suffer until it dissolves.

I know what you may be thinking... All this is good, but easier said than done. I would tend to agree, but one thing is for sure: none of this will work unless you first become conscious of what makes you suffer. It's one thing to suffer (we all know what this is like), but it's another thing to be conscious of it.

We have a very useful built-in system which can help us immensely to become conscious of what causes suffering in us: suffering itself. If you're suffering, if you're not in bliss, then look no further. This is the signal that there is something inside you that still needs to be adressed. So sit, breathe, and look. You will find that what is hurting are attachments that keep you chained to the bottom of your self-made dungeon, which in turn has been built with blocks and bricks of abandonmnent, rejection and guilt.

Please don't just read the lines above: let them sink. Re-read them and breathe into them, deeply. I am not asking you to blindly believe anything I write here, but I do ask you to at least give it a try. Actually, I don't really care that much if you do give the techniques a try or not (and yet, I do!), but one thing I know: if you give it a good try, even just once, then you won't need to believe me.

It won't be a *fact* anymore. It will become an experience. It will become a Truth. For you, not anyone else.

What Damn Dungeon and Chains?!
There Ain't None!

Why do we usually overlook our own emotions and attachments and instead try to soothe our suffering by looking outside of us? There's something we do, a defense mechanism that we have that we'll call *denial* (which I spoke of before). We deny that there is even a dungeon and chains to begin with, so it's hard to even begin to do something about it! As long as someone adopts a defensive stance and denies the suffering, nothing can really be done, except letting the intensity of the suffering build up until there is no other option than to take care of it.

But what are these denials? Again, like for the three broad types of emotions, there are three types of denials: fear, shame, and pride.

Denials are truly what keeps us blocked and attached. We are stuck because of our attachments in a fortress of emotions. When these emotions are freed by looking at them and breathing into them, happiness comes all by itself, because there's nothing to attach us away from it and nothing blocking us from it anymore.

I can't transmit happiness itself to you, but I can transmit information that will stimulate your own idea of how you could face your inner mechanisms preventing you from experiencing happiness. This process of looking inwards to face your own emotional clockwork is what we call integration. Although uncomfortable, integration is truly what I call comfortable suffering. Willingly sitting and observing an uncomfortable emotion for a short moment of time, say 5 to 15 minutes, until it loses its power over you is not always fun, but it is quite comfortable compared to being caught in an intense emotional turmoil in the heat of the moment.

So far, we have done two easy, but oh so useful, techniques. We have first done happy-facing: flooding ourselves with happiness. Then, I asked you to bring back a painful emotion (abandonment or rejection) from your past. Now, we'll take it a step further and do another short period of comfortable suffering. But first, I ask you to do a few minutes of happy-facing.

Done? Great.

Earlier, I asked you to pick a moment when you felt rejected, or abandoned. Now, I'll ask you to be a bit more courageous and pick a moment when you felt some level of guilt. In your teenage or adulthood, you most certainly have some memories of events that triggered guilt in you. Summon that feeling back. Think of the event, re-live it in your mind, and feel it. Breathe and sink down in the guilt like we did for abandonment and rejection, but again, without dramatizing it, without getting wrapped up in the theatrical scene. Without convincing yourself that you should or should not feel that guilt. Just feel it, objectively. Don't try to forgive it. Don't change it. Don't resolve it. Don't think about it rationally trying to find out where it comes from, etc. Just feel it. Feel what you felt back then- no more no less. You'll see that simply by sinking into it, it starts to lose it's power over you and it becomes information. Uncomfortable information I agree, but information nonetheless. Breathe deep into it... and relax.

It has to make you uncomfortable, but it doesn't need to be torture. It may not seem like it, but we're speaking about happiness right now, or at least, what pulls us out of it. All those weights that we carry in our heart and soul that make it impossible for simple hapiness to just arise for no reason. This is what we are learning about now so that we can have the tools, once and for all, to free ourselves and finally experience levels of happiness that we may never have thought possible. Breathe deep, relax your muscles, especially your diaphragm if you feel the emotion has a tight grip on you, and just let go...

It always takes us a while to take care of an experience of suffering in our life, because we're either ashamed, afraid, or too proud to admit it in the first place. The worst fear of all is the fear of being afraid, the worst shame is the shame of being ashamed and the worst pride is being proud of being proud.

Some very proud people I try to teach those techniques to sometimes tell me: "Oh yeah, so you think I'm proud, huh? Yeah okay, so I *am* proud. So what?! Fuck you!!" Okay, no problem at all. I'll go fuck myself. What else can I tell them? What else can I do? Some people are like that, blinded by their pride. They simply have to recognize themselves as being so proud that this is truly what hurts. Until they do, there's nothing else to be done.

But pride is not just a "bad guy". Pride is actually a legitimate defense mechanism that we cling to because it is meant to perpetuate life. Thanks to pride, shame, and fear, we're still alive as a species. However, because of that very same fear, shame, and pride, we also die in suffering and pain, usually after a long illness.

Denials are what make you refuse to look at an emotion. And what happens when you don't look at an emotion? Life pushes it out, forces it into your life. The same things keep happening. Painful situations happen over and over and over again. Each time they get stronger, more painful. Each time they intensify. Why is this? Because your soul is trying to tell you: "Look at it! Pay attention! Look, sit, breathe and exist NOW! This is suffering!"

Eventually, if you keep refusing to look at it, you'll find yourself in a situation where you have no choice, no issue, nowhere else to hide or run away. Stuck in a hospital bed. Unemployed. Emotionally badly hurt. Broke. Unable to bring back to life someone you loved who just died a few seconds ago. Life will find a way to tell you, "Look, this is suffering."

Among the many people I interact with all over the world, I meet a lot of people who so strongly believe in the "power" of their healing rocks, their blessed incense from that wonderful country, their statues of this or that divinity, etc. All trying to prove to me that they can avoid suffering thanks to their meditation and mindset, still refusing to admit that they suffer, still refusing to look at their suffering.

I usually ask them to be so kind the day they attain self-realization to accept me as their disciple. Then, after a few years, I sometimes hear back from them asking: "Hi, Maha... You remember way back when, there was this thing you told me about pride? Well, I was wondering if... What was it all about again?' Denials, my friends. Denials. Cunning as they may be.

Jesus said to Lazarus' sisters: "Why do you think the suffering is in vain? Don't you know my Father has a plan?" Yes, he did his little miraculous trick and resurrected Lazarus, but the miracle was not what the teaching was about. Of course, it was quite a show and it stuck in the mind of people. This is what went down in history books, but it misses the point completely.

Research and Development

The first thing that the Buddha said is that there are four truths, and I only truly grasped them through enlightenment:

The first one is: There is suffering.

The second truth in buddhism is: There is understanding of suffering.

The third truth in buddhist wisdom is: There is cessation of suffering. It just stops.

The fourth truth that the buddha taught: There is no suffering. There was simply an experience.

Just like anything else, to understand suffering, you have to study it. To study it you have to look at it. Again, we must be careful about the words we attach to experiences. We can't really *look* at an emotion, but we can *feel* it. The eyes are organs of perception on the physical level, while feeling is the organ of perception at the emotional level.

Why are we here? Why are we here trying to love and be loved? And why do we screw up?

Actually when you think that you screwed up something in life, please realize that it's nothing more than a misperception, a misundertanding of suffering. If you think of a past event which leaves you now with the feeling that you screwed up, please understand that you were really doing your best for you, at this time, under those circumstances. It may have been the wrong reaction, the wrong thing, done at the wrong time, but you did not screw up: you were doing research and development.

I mentioned that to understand suffering, we must look at it and study it. Imagine yourself being a scientist who's working on some new theory. "Let's see, what will happen if I do this... Oh no!!! Look what happened! I wanted to find a way to achieve something useful and instead of that, the whole lab exploded! It's not what I wanted, nor what I expected! I shouldn't have done this!"

Then you feel guilt and shame and your fellow scientists reject you, and you build blocks and stay attached, and the merry keeps going round and round to the sound of everything we talked about so far. This is nature. It's normal. So don't beat yourself over all this. There is a way beyond all that, and maybe your way of thinking and your actions were not the most agile, but there is nothing wrong with you at all! Yes, you suffer. But you're still alive. You were not evil. You were merely incompetent in trying to love in this way or in that way.

So, you find out overtime that kicking someone in the ass does not bring you a sense of love by others nor for others. It may have brought some sense of one-sided justice, but not love. Not what you're truly trying to achieve.

In denial, what the ego truly does is try to find a way to prevent you from understanding suffering. As you can see, it's not the most efficient way to free yourself and make you experience everlasting bliss, but that's the ego's way of working (the only way it knows). It's okay. Your ego is your best friend. It's not your enemy. Maybe you read somewhere that your ego is what makes you do all those evil things and that it has to be eradicated, but that's also a misunderstanding. The ego is the tool that allows you to do research and development. The ego is your best friend in that it wants what is best for you, and it's trying as hard as it can. It's just that it is somewhat incompetent.

Instead of looking at yourself as a bad person doing mistakes and feeling guilty about it, you could look at yourself as someone trying his or her best to love and be loved, and look upon yourself with self-love. Please note that I said *self-love*: not *self-esteem*, nor *self-confidence*, nor *self-appreciation*.

Because of denials, you may end up building low self-esteem for yourself, which of course is a cause of suffering. But because of those same denials, you can also build high self-esteem. This may not be quite as evident, but high self-esteem is also a cause of suffering.

In fact, the concept of esteem itself, regardless if it is high or low, is cause of suffering. High self-esteem, low self-esteem, it doesn't matter: esteem is a cause of suffering. As weird as this may sound, trying to have more self-trust, more self confidence, and more self-esteem will only make you suffer more.

Instead, try to get into the mindset that there is no concept of *worth* or of *worthlesness*. They don't exist. We create them and end up believeing in them. We don't have worth, nor value. What we have is love. We're not a piece of crap, nor are we a wonderful person. We're an experience of love. Period. This outlook on things is an infinitely more productive way to handle and process our experience in this world.

If you pretend to be a wonderful and great person, you'll end up hating yourself if you make a mistake. On the other hand, if you pretend to be a bad person, you'll hate yourself no matter what, even if you do good things. High and low self-esteem support and feed the concept of esteem in you, and you'll tend to evaluate everybody else through that concept as well. This will inevitably bring suffering because self-esteem is based on competition amongst other humans. It feeds off comparison. It is always pitted against other types of perceived *goodness* and perceived *badness* inside and outside. Comparison means separation. It's not Oneness. Separation leads to abandonment, rejection, and guilt.

So you have all these people trying to discover how worthy and wonderful they are when the only thing they truly want is to discover love. In truth, they don't want to know how wonderful they are: this is their ego at work. What they truly want is to be reassured that there is love.

Let this sink in for a minute. Re-read the last few paragraphs and feel them. Breathe deeply. Contemplate the wisdom. Become conscious that you don't have to be a performant human being. You don't have to be efficient in your self-therapy. Just do it at your own pace from the angle that separation, competition, and comparison are not unbiased options.

Some people go about in the world knowingly or unknowingly thinking in terms of, "I will be loved when they bow to me... I will be happy when he sees me, acknowledges me, reacts to me..."

What the heck is that other than a cause of suffering!? Sometimes we don't even know we do that (but we sometimes do) out of incompetence. We do it to our boss, our wife, our friends, our neighbors. And even if we know that we're doing it, most of us will never admit it. Being in denial about it doesn't change the fact that we do it.

Self-worth and worthlessness alone will not bring you very far in your research and development lab, in your quest to experience love. Compassion will be useful, but if you cannot be compassionate, at least be respectful. Start with that until you're ready to move on to higher wisdom.

I Could Be a Fraud,
However Your Experience is True

We've covered tons of information so far. Tons of stuff that triggered experiences in you. Hopefully, those triggered experiences in you are coming together and are beginning to make sense. You'll notice something (and those who have known me for a while or have attended many of my seminars, online or in person, will be able to confirm). I never talk about something saying that it's the truth. I only refer to experiences.

As a teaching tool, I'll often trigger something in people and then ask: "See what just happened? What did you just feel? What do you think? Look at it. Think about it." I'm not doing this in an effort to boost my own ego, nor in an effort to make you feel bad because I *discovered your dark little secret*. It is you that this is about, not me. I have my own *dark little secrets* as well. I've dissolved quite a lot, but I'm still living in this world, hence, I'm just as screwed as you are. I just have more experience than many in observing those patterns, and I share the wisdom. That's all.

All this is to trigger experiences in you and then guide you through the observing process so that you can more easily find your own path. Now you see that it doesn't matter if I'm enlightened or not. Who cares. I could be a fraud. It doesn't matter. What does matter is your experience, your own happiness.

What you experience is true. Not what you learn. What you experience is what brings you true wisdom. What you learn merely brings you knowledge. Don't get me wrong. Knowledge is very important. It's a great survival tool. But, it will not bring you the wisdom to deal with the emotional issues at their roots. Many very knowledgeable people are in great pain.

You don't have to trust me nor fear me on this. Trust your experience. This is how you should handle all your spiritual work. You can read tons of books, you can know by heart all the mantras and all the techniques, even read my own books and learn the mantras that I teach myself, but it will never bring you the wisdom that can be discovered by yourself through simply taking the time to look within your heart and observe: "So this is what I feel..."

While the human perceives information through the senses, the soul perceives only experiences. So when you take the time to allow the soul to contemplate "That hurts!", you'll quickly stop doing what is painful. And this process has nothing to do with rationalizing intellectually.

You can try to rationally convince yourself, "I'm going to stay in balance on my figurative bike!" by reading books, burning incense, playing new-agey psychedelic music... but unless you fall off your bike and hurt yourself first-hand, you won't truly understand. Your nervous system just won't participate.

Whatever you do in life, you will do things that bring you joy and you'll say to yourself, "Oh, that's a good thing to do." On the other hand, you'll also do things that will bring you pain and you'll think, "Ouch! That's not a good thing to do! Let's do more of the happy things!" As I mentioned, suffering alone is not going to bring you wisdom. If you consider only your experiences of suffering, you still won't get it. In fact, only pain will probably do quite a bit of damage and very little wisdom. You also need experiences of happiness for you to fiind balance.

Some of you who are reading this book have been through so much happiness and suffering in your life that maybe generating new experiences is not really what you need right now. Maybe a wiser approach would be to simply use the raw data you already have. As you read this, most of you already have plenty of densified emotions and plenty of wall building around you. You already have a lot of things to integrate and work with to bring back inside what is outside.

If you're disturbed by what someone has told you in the past, this is an excellent place to start. 'She told me I was a moron! He told me I was stupid!" What hurts is not what was said. It's the belief that what was said is true. Integrate it. Bring this inside of you. Realize that what the other person says does not have power over you. The only thing that has power over you is your own interpretation of what you perceive. So, if someone tells you you're a wonderful person, pride grows and that person affects you. I agree that the way in which it affects you is positive, but that person is still affecting you- creating ripples within you.

When our ego is flattered in what we perceive as a good way (such as when someone tells us how wonderful we are), instead of bringing this inside of us, we have a tendency to tell ourselves: "Oh, I so much love this person! Any and everyone who thinks I'm wonderful, I love them all!"

However, I tell you this: ask yourself if you truly are wonderful. What would you feel if you felt the experience without letting the mind's value system interfere? If you truly got to the core of it, you'd feel love. Go to the core of the experience, you'll see it has nothing to do with value, or being *wonderful,* and it has everything to do with love. Value is in the mind. Don't let your mind trick you.

But, in order to be able to fully become conscious of this, one has to look within; whereas, our ego is built to convince us that the solution is outside. Looking within feels a little bit against nature, especially at first. So not only are we seeking solutions outside of ourselves, but since carrying all those emotions within us is painful at times, many prefer to pretend they don't have them to begin with.

"I have no emotions!" Okay, so you have no emotions. Then, 10 years later, you still don't have emotions, but you have a cancer, you broke both of your legs, you crashed your car. Whatever you pretend not to have or feel will find a way to make you pay attention. It is going to be projected outside. It will run after you. This is how the soul works: by getting into your human and radiating its experience.

So, now it should be clear that emotions densify into a complex network of filters and blocks. So, when the love of your soul manages to shine through and reaches you, of course it has been all tainted by those screens and shields- by those emotions that are clogged there. This is why it is very useful to take time to go suffer consciouly and comfortably. Don't torture yourself, but realize that you will not find happiness until you take a moment in your life to honestly tell yourself: "Okay, I'm suffering now. It doesn't feel good at all. I loved this beautiful brand new car so much and now this imbecile scratched it And I suffer. What a jerk! What a jerk!"

At one point, you will come to understand that you're not suffering because of the perceived jerk outside, but because of your own attachment to the brand new car. You suffer because of something in you lures you into giving the outside power over you. If you try to fix whatever is outside that affects you, you're running up a dead-end street. If you end up succeeding in preventing all the jerks in the world from scratching your car (which you will never achieve anyhow), your soul will find another way to show you what the real issue is. And the real issue is inside. Fix what is inside.

The only legitimate suffering we have is only if someone threatens our life. If someone puts a gun to your head, he might actually have the power to impose suffering on you. But if someone "offended" your car, you can still drive it. I know, it's not fun to have a bump or a scratch on our beloved car, but how willing are you to let that make you mad and unhappy? Is it really worth it? Once the car is scratched, what else can you do?

If someone scratches my car, the only thing I can do is have it repaired. That's it! Nothing else. No other reaction is needed nor useful! A scratch on a car is not dramatic. There's a scratch, and I think it would look better without it, so I go to the body shop and have it patched. And, that's the end of it.

I could be mad and suffer and repair my car; or I could be happy and repair my car. When you think about it, who in their right mind would willingly want to be all upset if the end result is the exact same? I know that the scratch on my car won't prevent me to eat, won't put a gun on my head, won't deprive me of my shelter, nor my clothes, and that my family is still safe. Where's the problem?!

I have a question for you: Do you eat everyday? Do you have clothes to wear? Do you have a shelter? Yes? You live in a home somewhere, you have a roof, right? You're not exposed to icy cold storms and suffocating dry heat? Nobody is threatening your life right now at this moment? So basically, you have everything it takes to be happy. All that you need to stay alive, you got it.

Everything else is a dream.

Reality Exists but Illusions
are More Efficient

Buddhists often say, "Everything is an illusion." However, that is not what the Buddha said. The original saying was more in the line of, "Everything that you perceive is an illusion." He didn't say that the chair you sit on is not real, but he did say that what you perceive of it is an illusion.

Let's use a table as an example. The table is real, but it's not a table. The concept *table* is the illusion. If a bunch of kids came running by the table and hid under it, it would become a shelter. This is how easily something can lose it's properties and identity. Simply by using something in a different way than was originally intended by the builder changes it's function. So if the function of a table is to support things, sit at to eat, etc., and that function can be easily changed to protect something, the concept *table* is fabricated and impermanent. If something can change function, it's concept is illusory. It's useful perhaps to be efficient in everyday life, but illusory nonetheless.

So if a table is not a table, what could it be? In what way could we describe it so that the definition could always apply no matter what the circumstances? Well, if you wanted to get to the core of what this is, you could say that it's matter, made of wood shaped in a certain way. Of course, I understand that it is used to put stuff on it and that we have labelled it *table* for efficiency's sake, but whether used as a shelter or a table, you can pretty much be certain that it will always be wood and steel matter...or...can you really be so sure?

Suppose I want you to put a glass of water on the table. Of course, I'm not going to say, "Please, can you put this transparent cylinder sealed at one end that contains a liquid substance that I drink on this flat surface made of hard organic matter supported by four 30 inch legs..." I'll simply say, "Can you put the glass of water on the table please."

We need to be efficient in our communication if we are to get anything done, so we use words that refer to more complex concepts. But because we need to be efficient in our communication, we forgot what was reality and we end up taking for granted that this is a table. But, since it can stop being a table just by a snap of the fingers, we can't really say that *table* is the core nature of this object.

So, it's not a table. It's wood. Bu,t could that change? Is wood permanent and changeless? What happens if you throw the wooden table in a furnace? It would become some other kind of matter, right? What does this leaves us with now?

Well, first, we realized that this is not a table. That it is matter. And, that the term table is merely a label we use to describe it's current shape and function. Then, we also discovered that we cannot even call it wood either, because under high enough temperatures that *matter* will simply give off a lot of it's energy and be transformed into something else. It seems to be matter, because it's solid and appears to stand still to us. In reality it's made of energy, which modern science now can prove without a shadow of a doubt using measuring tools way more powerful than our own crude senses.

So, it's not a table, and it's not even matter because even this is still some level of illusion. So, if we truly refine our perception, we'll discover that what is not a table, nor matter, is energy compounded into something that appears to stand still. Why is it standing still? Because it remembers it's place. It has a form of memory of it's properties. Furthermore, if this energy remembers something, then it's mind.

This is also what the Buddha said, "All of reality is mind". But, there's another trap there. Many Buddhist go about saying that reality is in your mind, which is *not* the case. Just as he said that what one *perceives* is an illusion (and not that everything *is* an illusion), he also said that all of reality *is* mind (and not that all of reality is *in your* mind).

Everything is thought that gave properties to energy and collapsed it, fixed it, settled it in a certain way And then you have the laws of nature interfering with it all. I will stress this once more:

The Buddha did not say, "Everything is an illusion. Reality is in your mind."

He said, "Everything you perceive is an illusion. Reality is mind."

What you perceive through your senses is an illusion, but what we call *table* is nevertheless real because you can experience it. You can feel it under your knuckles if you punch it. You can hear the sound it makes. There is indeed something there which appears to our crude senses as solid matter.

You can go sit in a cave for 20 years and stare at a pebble on the ground and wait for enlightenement to come. It may happen. Some people did it. But, you can also still be here and enjoy your car, your family, your friends, and your job. You can still entertain yourself. You can keep playing with the sources of suffering and of happiness. Eventually, overtime, you will find an experience of immovable bliss, or enlightenment, or everlasting happiness. Call it whatever you want. You will eventually stop being affected by illusions. You will stop being affected by people who call you an asshole, or by the jerk who scratched your car. This immovable bliss-this enlightenment- is the one and only thing that will happen to you without a doubt, in this lifetime or a future one.

Reality is What you Experience.
Illusion is How you Interpret it.

As I mentionned earlier, truth is an experience. It has to do with what one feels. Information is knowledge. It has to do with facts. Truth has nothing to do with facts or information. It has to do with experience.

2 + 2 equals 4: That's a perception. Of course, 4 seems to be the only possible result stemming from 2 + 2 in the system that we were taught and collectively use. And, for efficiency's sake, we're still going to use the system. It would be dumb to reject the wisdom that is so useful for us in our societies, and that we have "packaged" into various workable systems which we use and need. But, if we want to free ourselves from suffering, we still have to recognize those systems for what they are- no less, but no more.

Let's talk about one such system, which is an illusion and has power over many of us. A common way to represent this system is to draw a circle and divide it in segments, draw lines on its outer edge, affix numbers to those lines and have arrows spinning and pointing to them. If the arrows don't match the right moments for you to do, or not to do, certain things the network of other systems, and the people who rely on those systems, will try to make you feel bad, will try to make you feel that *you* are bad. It may get to the point where you feel hated, or maybe even hate yourself! Oh, yes, indeed, you're going to feel a lot of mixed emotions if you don't go along with that system!

Of course you understand that I am referring to the system of Time. How much power do we give to our schedule? How much power does it have over us? As you can see, there are causes of suffering in the system we call time. But why did we come up with that system to begin with? Because if having to put up with schedules causes suffering, not having them causes more of it.

Again, as it applies for words in our communication, the goal of having a system allowing us to keep track of what is past and future, was for us to be efficient. So it's wise to keep using it, but it doesn't mean that you are guilty of something if you don't obey to it. You don't have to feel bad, nor feel that you are bad, if you don't fit in the system. The system was built for us to be more efficient in society, but please be conscious of the power we give it over our emotional state. *That's* the illusion.

Please take a moment to breathe deeply as you re-read three previous paragraphs, as you contemplate them and truly feel them.

So, how do we free ourselves from systems? Please understand that by this, I do not mean how can we work around the system, avoid the system, or beat the system. I am talking about how to free ourselves from it, while still using it to our best advantage.

To free yourself from the system, the first thing you have to do is to stop running away. Remember that you use time as a means to be efficient. At work, everybody arrives at the same time and people obey the rules, which avoids chaos. You may not like the system, but you'll discover a lot more suffering by revolting against it than to simply go along with it.

For example, traffic lights are arranged into a system that we created to commute safely. If you don't stop at every red light, something may happen to remind you that no matter how much you hate the system, maybe you should have respected it. But, a red light by itself does not have the power to stop your car and it certainly has no power over you. It merely suggests that you should, on your own, do something about it. The light itself is just information. It is you who has to decide what is the truth in that. The truth can be either "I'm still alive waiting for the light to turn green", or it can also be "I'm dead, but fuck it, I fought the system!" Ultimately, it's your choice. That's one example illustrating my point when I talk about research and development.

So, you want to fight the system? You are free to do so, and discover the suffering that will inevitably result. Or, are you enslaved to the system? Well, you can choose to be, and also discover the suffering that stems from this approach. The wise stance is to use the system for the best it can bring you, but to stop perceiving it as having any kind of power over you: this is purely illusory.

Let's take another example, another system: Authority. As a system, authority is even older than the system of time (even if that one has been around for quite a while already). Are you obeying your boss to avoid him or her being mad at you? Do you have a symbol of authority in your life that you think has power over you? Again, the solution is not to flee away from that perceived authority, nor to confront it, just to establish some sort of position for yourself. You'll quickly realize that this also carries it's own charge of suffering.

The solution is simply to evolve your perception about it. If your boss gives you money because you willingly do what he asks of you, you're just doing business. It's a transaction- nothing more, nothing less. You are free to enact according to instructions, and those instructions are not orders. You're not enslaved in a way that you must follow orders, or be fired if you don't. That's misperception.

Do your best to follow the instructions to the best of your ability so that the boss can do his or her best to give you what he's supposed to give you in this system: money. The solution is not to fight the system nor flee from it.

The solution is to readjust your perception about it and free yourself, not from what you perceive as the cause of suffering outside (namely your job), but from your own inner beliefs.

If you flee away from the system, you're in denial, being either "too proud" to obey, or "ashamed" of something you did wrong, or "afraid" of your boss reaction. Whatever denial you use, if you flee, you'll simply have to find another job, and after the initial few weeks of excitment has worn off, when you get back in the 9 to 5 groove, you're going to find yourself in a situation very similar to the one you fleed from, because your inner mechanisms are still in place and your soul will think: "I still did not understand how to stay in balance. Let's try again."

So, what's the solution? It's to stop perceiving your boss as having power over you. The solution is to look at the shame or the pride you have inside, of the fear you have of other's judgement. You're afraid of being abandoned if your boss doesn't like you. Your boss is a symbol of authority and you were trained by your parents to react in this or that way towards authority. So you unconsciously go back to the pattern that you learned as a kid through the relationship you had with your parents.

The exact same thing can be said if you have a hard time dealing with police officers. "Oh I hate those bastards! They gave me a ticket!" Do you still think that your parents were spanking you when you were young because they hated you? Please see this: They rather most likely gave you a bit of suffering in hoping that you would avoid stronger suffering later. They gave you a little correction now in hoping to make you avoid major corrections later on. Yes, I know some parents cross a certain line and simply use this as an excuse to beat up their kids (they have their own cause of suffering and they impose it on their kids). I understand the suffering in that. But I'm talking about the general principle of how they're trying their best to love you even if they are being incompetent. They're no better or worse than you. They're also doing research and development.

Compassion is understanding that we're all doing our best. If a woman beater would truly know the experience he's imposing to others, he would stop immediatly. But, it's not legal to beat up someone who's physically violent, so don't, even if you feel the urge to. If you do, you'll have the whole legal system come down on you telling you that you have no business to kick the ass of the ass kicker.

Oh, I know. This legal system that is supposedly made to prevent suffering is not perfectly suited to all situatons. I understand that. But it has been put in place exactly because without it, on average, it would be even worse. It may not be perfect, but you'd probably suffer even more if it wasn't there.

So just take care of yourself, of your own experience. Ask yourself what hurts you inside: "He called me a bitch! He fired me from my job! He gave me a ticket! He made a scratch on my car! They're morons! All of them!" I am asking you this: What are you attached to? Self-worth? Physical value of things? Aesthetics? Money? Others' judgements of you? What's the emotion you feel? Is it abandonment, rejection or guilt?

You now have the main key components to resolve your own trials in life. You don't need to intellectually understand them, just simply sit in the suffering and observe it. Notice I said "sit and observe" the suffering. I didn't say "support" the suffering. Some people play the victim. They suffer from abandonment, and they pile some more suffering on top, waiting and hoping for a savior. That's ego also, that's a cause of suffering. Eventuallly they'll see that playing the victim doesn't truly bring satisfaction, it doesn't bring them happiness. So consciously, not dramatically, sit in your emotion and feel it.

If you feel it helps you, you can jot a few notes on paper and destroy the pages afterwards. Just put your feelings in words if it's easier for your mind to grasp. Sometimes it's good to write key points. Notice I said *key points*, not the entire story in all it's details! If you end up with 15 pages of prose, you're not feeling your emotions, you're writing a novel! Keep it simple, use key words as reminders. For example: "Jerk made a scratch on car. I blew a fuse. I felt abandoned."

When the emotion is there, breathe into it for as long as it takes for it to fade. As I mentionned earlier, once you are done observing the unpleasant emotion, don't just stop the process there. Don't remain with that uneasy feeling within you. Fill yourself with joy in the same way I explained earlier in this book. See every part of you, down to the tiniest of cells, as happy faces. Once you have filled yourself with joy and happiness to "wash off" the painful residue left from your observation, then you can go about your usual business.

Part 2

It Hurts but It's for Your Own Good

One of the most important things in one's life is to know what to do with all those experiences that are so confusing. Keeping balance while handling the sufffering and the happiness is something that is important to know. I could be saying a lot of great things, but I advise you not to take my word for it. There are things I teach that seem so weird only because not many people have talked about it to the public, meaning that many have been kept secret, or taught only to a selected few. However, please consider this: Why should these great teachings, that can help increase happiness, be kept secrets in esoteric temples and hidden from those who so much need them?

The Buddha said on his deathbed: I have thaught everything exoteric and esoteric, secret and public alike, because it would be arrogant for a teacher to keep wisdom from a student that so needs it to resolve suffering.

Esoteric doesn't mean that I should keep something secret because I'm better than you. This would imply a sense of value, a sense of worth, and we saw earlier how this concept, which exists only in our own mind, creates suffering. Esoteric simply means that it is better for me not to tell you because it's going to promote suffering if I do.

So, precisely *because* of that, precisely *because* I know it's going to hurt if I tell you this esoteric wisdom, I *am* teaching it and have been for a while: go sit in suffering, even if it's so uncomfortable that you'd be glad to revert to your protective, anesthetizing ignorance. However, as I mentionned, don't stop there. After having sit in suffering, make a point of sitting in happiness.

That's what esoteric is. It doesn't mean that this wisdom shouldn't be revealed to you, it only means that you need to be prepared to hear it. Then, you need to remember that you have a free mind. You need to go home and decide for yourself if you are going to apply and study this wisdom or not. This must not be imposed upon you. A free will and a free mind by their very nature never have to obey. Please respect the wisdom, but never ever feel obliged to submit to it. Remember that no matter how spiritually advanced someone is, other people have absolutely no power over you. I certainly don't, so don't listen to me. Don't obey me. You are free.

You were born butt naked. You didn't have a sofa, a laptop, and a BMW when you came into existence. You were empty-handed, and when you leave this world at the end of your present experience, you won't take anything you currently think you own with you. So yeah, I'm going to give you esoteric wisdom: Death teaches us something.

Death teaches that you have no possessions, no relationships, no identity. When I visit a country to give seminars, I like to play with the identity of the people who attend, especially when they're proud of it. So, you're American, English, French, Spanish, Australian or Thai, and you're proud about that? You identify tightly with your country and it's citizens?

Well, some day you're going to die and be born in China, Norway, Poland, Mexcico or Morroco, so that you can understand that you are neither American nor Chinese, neither French nor Mexican. Free your mind from identity. We all currerntly live somewhere that we have collectively agreed to define with words, and geometrical and geographical concepts for efficiency's sake. Had I been born a thousand years ago, or a thousand years from now, in exactly the same place, that place would be named something else and I would probably speak another language and be identified as a "Whateveran". But to be efficient, we use words and a variety of systems so yes, in that system, I am Canadian. But my human nationality has abolutely no value outside that system.

If you want to be free from the pain of death, if you want it to be a wonderful experience, if you want to die peacefully and not after years of anguish and suffering, you need to learn the teachings of death before it happens. Detach from posessions, detach from the people you love, and get rid of your identity. Again, detaching doesn't mean to get rid of. Do not get rid of your possession: detach from them. It means have fun while they're there, and not to hang on when they have to go away.

Cut those attachments to people and to material things. Have fun with them, but when they have to go, be efficient in your suffering and let them go. If I were mourning someone right now, I'd go sit in abandonment and really feel it deep down for 3 days, and then be done with it. I wouldn't want to take 3 years to get over something or someone if I can do it efficiently in 3 days.

Do you understand the deeper meaning of what I'm saying here? **Enjoy, then let go.** Objects, situations, people, landscapes, holidays, hobbies...be happy while they're there and stay happy when they're gone. Remember that true happiness is the one you feel for no reason, so it has nothing to do with their presence. It all has to do with being happy because you want to. Simply remember that all those things are like side dishes, not the main meal.

The only thing I suggest to completely get rid of is your identity. Your identity is made of your geographic, linguistic, cultural, racial, and many other attachments. It's also made of your preferences. Preferring the taste of strawberry over that of chocolate, whatever your culture is. You need to get to the point where you can have preferences, but remain free from them. When you can't eat something because you find it to be too gross, please see that this stems from the fact that there are other things that you love so much and you're attached to them, hence other things disgust you. Because of the happiness you think you find outside, you get suffering that seems to come from outside. It's the same thing. Detach from what you prefer and you will no longer be bothered by what you dislike. Again, it doesn't mean to give up what you enjoy: just detach from it, so that what you dislike doesn't affect you as much, if at all. If you detach from what makes up your human identity, you can still use that identity because it's fun, but you won't be enslaved to it.

I understand that this is a challenge. It's not so easy to let go of what we think we own. Some people tell me: "I worked so hard to get a house, it's going to stay mine until I die no matter what you say or how you say it!" Yes, yes, yes... I understand. It's your house. It is the place where you live. Nevertheless, if anyone comes to affect it, you're going to suffer. Yet, all you'd have to do if it was damaged would be to repair it- no more no less. The same thing applies to anything you own and every person you interact with.

Many years ago, a guy went to a party. For some reason he had a gun with him. I was 18, and my brother was 19. The guy took the gun and shot my brother at point-blank range. By the way, this is not a metaphor, it's a true story. As you might expect, my brother died.

When I got home, I went to my room, sat there and observed the pain and the separation I felt. I just sat there motionless. I remember saying, "O Mother! It hurts so much, come and take me in your arms!" I'm not speaking of my biological mother. I was waiting for Holy Mother Mary to take me because I felt so alone that I would not make it. I asked her to take me within her. "Take me in you, I love you. This is just too painful!"

Three days later, as the tradition goes, the body of my brother was exposed just before his official funerals. The guy who had shot him decided to come. At the party when he killed my brother, the guy was under the influence of some kind of substance, and he just wanted to see for himself that this was not a joke, that he didn't dream the events three days earlier and that this was real. He couldn't believe it, it had to be a dream. It had to be just a joke. He had to see the dead body to fully understand the extent of his action.

So as he came closer, I moved away and allowed him to pass, so did my parents. So, the guy going in front of the body of my brother can now understand that this is absolutely not a joke, nor a dream. He cries a bit. He's still the same guy, with his good and bad sides so to speak, but he cries humbly, acknowledging what he had done. After a couple of minutes, he gets back up and my father goes over to him and says, "It's now time for you to go." My father is enlightened by the way. You don't have to take my word for it, but it's part of the true story.

So as the guy is just about to leave, I hurry towards him and jump on him. Everybody was certain that I was going to beat him up. But I don't. I take him in my arms, I firmly hug him and say, "I want you to live your life knowing I forgive you. You need to live your life knowing there is forgiveness!" I said it loud enough for everyone around to hear and realize that this was compassion and that it's possible. This is not just a story in the Bible or in a sutra. This is something that one can truly live by.

But how could I manage to do that only three days later? Was I in denial, was I afraid of the guy? No. I was able to do it because I faced it and consciously stayed in the suffering, observing and feeling it, until it was over. So when I hugged the guy and told him there was forgiveness, I was in a state of grace. I was at a point where I was not only able to take care of my suffering, but I also was able to care for the killer's own suffering. I'm not saying that you have to do that; I'm simply telling you that it is possible to experience such compassion to the point where nothing can have power over you, even the death of your loved ones. There is a way to be beyond that. Please contemplate this. Sink in the knowing that there is a way beyond that. Take a short moment to let this idea permeate through you while you breathe deeply and softly.

Ask a 2 year old child to sit still for 15 minutes without moving. After 5 minutes they'll start jumping all over the place. Then, ask a 75 year old person to sit still for 15 minuts, and it will be no problem at all. Why is that so?

One of the most obvious reasons is the ratio of 15 minutes vs total current lifespan. 15 minutes compared to two years is a different proportion of time than 15 minuts compared to 75 years. When you awaken spirituality and remember yourself as an immortal soul, existing in a reference of eternity in time, your entire lifespan here will seem insignificant. The soul that manifested through my brother back then is manifested as my first child today. That whole event when I was 18 didn't mean that it was over, nor that it was dramatic.

Of course, such events have to be prevented. You can't allow murderers to kill just because it's not dramatic in the grand scheme of things. The guy who shot my brother had to go to jail, and he did. He came out of jail still an asshole. Granted, he perhaps he came out with a little more reasearch and development under his belt, but still an asshole.

Two years later, I had found a job in a Subway, and he came in to get a sub sandwich, not knowing I worked there. I told my boss: "I want to be the one who makes his sub sandwich." When she asked me why. I replied, "Because he killed my brother two years ago, and I want to be the one who serves him."

My boss was a little baffled by this. She didn't know what I was going to do! She couldn't comfortably handle that kind of situation, so she stayed close to the telephone in case something went wrong.

But I had absolutely no plan to cause trouble. In fact, I'm smiled all along. "So how's your life now?" I asked the guy, while making his sub sandwich. "Are you alright? Did you go back to school or something?". I made sure to put a little bit more of every topping he asked for, trying to make the best possible sub for this guy. Because there's no better demonstration of compassion than that coming from someone whom you take for granted should tear your head off. I didn't want to harm him. Far from it! I took extra care of him and his order, including all those nice little extras, which he didn't pay for.

All the employees including the boss, were a little stunned. Like I said, my manager was right next to the phone waiting to call the police. After all, it was prudent of her, as she didn't know me that much at the time. I could have been a trouble maker. There was no way for her to know this.

But if you can remove yourself from the immediate events, please see that people hear these kinds of stories, including the family, friends and relatives, and people begin to evolve. Then, they think of a time when someone hurt their sister, their kids, their wife or their husband, and they start to think

"What am I going to do with this? Maybe rage and anger is not the only alternative at my disposal."

I told you that story, first of all because those events did happen. You can look it up in newspapers if you want. It's been written in a local newspaper that I forgave the guy who killed my brother. The interviewer said, "What? Um... Can I write this!?"

"Of course!" I said. "Yes, please do. Spread the word."

I don't encourage this kind of disastrous behavior, nor do I encourage suffering of course, but when suffering does come and when it's inevitable, don't fight it. When it comes, look at it and do what you can responsibly do to resolve it, but not by fighting in denial, in anger, in rage. Just be responsible and get back to a state of happiness as efficiently as you can.

You will have no choice at one moment or another in your life to sit, stop, suffer consciously, and breathe for the amount of time that it takes for the suffering to dissolve. Every one of your mournings happened this way, either in one shot or in fragments.

It doesn't mean I had to become friends with this killer. It means that I understand that it wasn't an offence, but reaserch and development very well disguised *as* an offence. If the only reference of perception is your normal human limited reference, you will not be able to conceive going beyond normal human reactions. This is why we learn spiritual techniques, which can be considered as completely whacky by some outsiders. We breathe, we imagine smiles and happy faces everywhere, we sit in suffering while doing nothing else but feel it... We do stuff to awaken the soul, which is what we truly are, we start perceiving beyond the senses, and then the illusions stop to have power over us. All this is pretty weird to those not open to spiritual evolution. Little do they know that they go thru exactly the same processes, intermittently, in small increments. It just takes more time. It's a process. You will have no choice, you'll have to go through it. You only get to choose at what pace.

If you don't like reading about those kinds of things, you're totally free to put those books down, not caring about it and continue to think it's a load of rubbish. Then, someday, stuff will impose this suffering on you because that's how life works, and maybe then you'll wish you had the tools we present you here to deal with the situation. In short, if you don't want the bad stuff to happen, you need to take care of the emotional state before it densifies and becomes a physical experience.

How You Influence Manifestation

What you are inside is constantly being projected in your life. It always works like that. This is how you manifest, and not through wishful thinking, positive affirmations and what-not. The theory exposed in the movie *The Secret* works with those who have no inner conflict, but you never hear about the 90% of people who just tried it with absolutely no results. There's something more than seeing the world through pink glasses in the process of manifestation.

You need to be able to exist in a state of being that is pure, free from emotional clogs. Only then will light come in and create whatever you want. This is how it works. That's how you influence movement of matter with your mind. In fact, this is exactly what everybody is already doing! But since they don't know the clockworks under the hood, things seem to manifest randomly in their lives, but believe me: it is anything but random.

This applies to absolutely everything, including bringing back to life someone who was dead when it's possible and the conditions are right. If the body is destroyed, you can try resurrection all you like. It won't work. When my first son was one years old, he poisoned himself with a berry called lily of the valley. It's the kind of berry that can induce a heart attack and kill an adult within a few hours. It had been 3 hours since my kid ate that thing, and he died.

On the moment of death, I summoned him back to life, because everything in his body was still in working condition, the body was not destroyed, and the soul still wanted to be there. But that's not resurrection. It's just a reboot. When people went to Jesus after such a miracle and said, "You resurrected him!"

Jesus simply said, "No, I just woke him up."

There's something called pre-mortem lethargy. It's a lethargy before the actual death when all the cells are still functional. It's just the organism as a single unit, as a whole, that doesn't work. Today, doctors call it reanimation. After twenty minutes, someone can be dead and electroshocks may reboot that person back to life.

When a car has stalled, it can sometimes run again by pushing it down a hill. The same thing can be done with a body. There's a way to do that. It's medically proven that this process can sometimes take place up to 12 hours after the individual has "died". There are documented cases where this happened. It's quite impressive, but it does happen. It's recorded in medical records.

However, to do this without the availablity of adequate equipment, using only willpower, the person doing it has to be totally free inside, free of emotional blocks and chains, free of fear, of attachments. If you're afraid of death, no matter how much or how hard you try to bring someone back to life, the body will remain dead as a way to tell you: "Look, look at it. You're afraid of death, look at it. You're attached and emotionally disturbed. You're attached to this person. You don't want to lose him or her. Feel the abandonment." It strangely resonates like the emotional integration process we're talking about, doesn't it?

There exists a very intensive process to free yourself, so that you can then play in life and have such supernatural abilities. And by the way, the term "supernatural abilities" is a misnomer. Any and all abilities are natural abilities, or else they wouldn't exist. It's just that science hasn't managed to discover them yet, it's not magic. But humans have been calling anything they couldn't understand "magic" or "superrnatural", and modern men are no better than their cavemen brothers when it comes to what is not yet understood.

That being said, let's suppose we can all get over on the fact that superrnatural is in fact *undiscovered natural*. Let's say that it is indeed magic, and that it refers to what exists in nature but does not yet have a reference in our scientific stack of knowledge. That could be called magic. Anything that you don't understand has been labelled as being magic, and thus doesn't exist naturally. At least, this is what many think. But, the reality is that we're just not there yet. Stuff is being explained now through quantum physics that seems to be taken straight from a fantasy book. Quantum physics is a very rich and interesting field of study. It points to the fact that there are many, many possibilities. It uncovers "magic". It strives to understand the "supernatural". I love it.

You're Chosen, They're Chosen, We're All Chosen

Why do certain people believe that it is essential that all these wonderful teachings, allowing one to free oneself and exist as a spiritual being, should be hidden by great, grand, pot-bellied masters with long beards, hidden somewhere in the mountains of Buthan? Why could it not be accessible right here, right now!? This is what I dedicate much of my life to, and some are not very happy about it. But I am more concerned about *all* rather than *some*.

Even if you could read and remember by-heart a hundred New-Age books, there would still be something missing to get a true profound spiritual experience. To get to that experience, you need just that: Experience. So, flipping pages, hearing audio tracks, and watching nicely packaged reports and documentaries will bring you a lot of intelligence, knowledge, charts and structure, making you very good at conceiving abstract concepts with your intellect. But you'd be not much further. You'd be knowledgeable, but you'd still suffer. The soul exists beyond the intellect, so it really doesn't matter that much what you read, hear, see or study. If there is no experience to back everything up, it's pointless. I know that it's fun to understand stuff with the mind, this is why I'm explaining all this to you. But it's only through objective observation and non-judgmental experience, not fantasy nor logic, that you will experience the Truth.

An example of an objective observation is the child trying to stay in balance on the bike that we spoke about earlier. Until the kid falls and experiences the pain of it first hand, he won't understand the importance of staying in balance.

I use metaphors to explain to you that it's by looking at life consciously that this wisdom is revealed. I am not talking about rationally looking at events with your intellect, using logic, I truly mean conscious observation. I have observed many people who thought they would be shielded from suffering by their self-confidence, and they still suffered. Then I looked at people with low or no self-esteem, and they also suffered. It is when people finally understand, after many years of trial and error (or a few hours of conscious observation), that there is no esteem, there is only Love... Ah! Then they become happy! Anyone can get to this wisdom. In fact, this is the only option! Eventually, enlightenment and immovable bliss is the only possible outcome, whether through conscious observation or through much suffering, and *not* through some divine gift from the heavens which would be given only to the Chosen One, or Chosen Ones.

First of all, what's this farce, The Chosen? We're supposed to be One, all of us! We're supposed to be in a state of Oneness. How can a small elite be free and not everybody else? Because they're chosen? Because they're better? Because they hold the truth?! What a joke! A joke that some think is true, but a joke nonetheless!

If you asked the supposedly Chosen Ones to give you their "secrets', they'd tell you that they can't do it since it's a gift from God. That only the Chosen can have it and that, since you're not chosen, you can't have it. Excuse my French, but this is utter bullshit! The reason why they can't give it to you is not because they're chosen, nor because it is some mystic gift from God himself to a selected few. No: the real reason why they can't give it to you is because it's an experience, and nobody can give you experience! You have to gain it yourself! There's nothing more to it! No Chosen, no gift, no joke, and no mystery. Only experience.

You'll have to just take a break and look at your life now and then, and try to be objective in your observations. You'll have to try to re-think everything outside the box and re-consider what they told you was the Truth. You'll be insecure, you'll be afraid of the unknown. It's Okay. It's all good. By now, you know how to deal with pain, discomfort and fear. Go sit and breathe into them.

You'll get to a point where you'll feel like you're falling. That's excellent. It may freak you out to realize that you have nothing to hold onto, like your human identity, your preferences, your relationships. None of that will help you out. Eventually you'll understand that, even with nothing to hold onto, you're not falling from anywhere, nor towards anything. You'll soon get to a point where you don't feel like you're falling anymore. This is the point where you'll know you are free, at peace within the illusion of turmoil. And then you'll understand that unknown doesn't mean fear: it means freedom. Freedom to think, freedom to observe, freedom to reevaluate everything. Not enslaved in an oppressive system.

You need to get to a point in your life knowing that you don't have to obey some kind of master. I'm not your master. I'm *a* master. What is a master? Someone who masters something. Some people are very good at cooking, others at driving cars, making movies, sing, tell jokes, act, and whatever else humans do nowadays. Not me. My mastery is spiritual evolution. I happen to have a knack for it. I understand it. I love it. I master it. It's my field of work.

If you want to learn how to cook, you can learn with a chef that's a master at cooking. Or, if you like, you can learn with grandma. It will work, eventually. After 20 years. But, if you want to become a chef, you need to study with a chef; or do 6,000 years of research and development in cooking by your own self to get to the same level of expertise. A chef has just accumulated wisdom on good and appropriate ways to cook a lot of things. So trust the chef and get there in 2 or 3 years. Good cooking is possible for those who take the time to study with those who have experience and knowledge to transfer. If you want to experiment cooking on your own, forget the chef and forget grandma. You're going to make something good eventually. There's no dramatic result of doing it alone.

If you don't want to study with a reliable source of spiritual wisdom, it's not dramatic either. You're going to make it. You don't absolutely need a master, it's just useful. A master doesn't have any power over others. Those who pretend to have a double agenda. They're charlatans. If a master is going to teach you how to become a master yourself, he cannot enforce the concept of attachment towards him, not even for himself. This is what I teach to my disciples.

I use the word "my disciples" because it's a useful and efficient label to refer to them in a certain way. But they're not truly my disciples. They're disciples, without the concept of relationship and possessivity, without the attachment. They're in a mindset of getting wisdom. The difference between a student and a disciple is that a student understands wisdom with his rational mind, whereas a disciple will feel the experience of being in Love. Not "in love" with the master: just in Love, without definition nor object.

In the same line of thinking, let's suppose that you want to learn how to fly. If you don't learn from an experienced pilot, you're only going to do a single attempt at research and development on your path to learn how to fly

There are more serious consequences to trying to learn to fly compared to trying to bake an apple pie by yourself. A whole bunch of people died in order to write the manual on how to stay alive while flying. It's that same manual, painfully put together over many years, that modern pilots now use in order to teach it to newbies how not to kill themselves gliding over cities and countries.

In that sense, doing spiritual work on your own has a risk threshold somewhere between learning to cook and learning to fly on your own. You won't kill yourself if you explore spirituality on your own, but you may hurt yourself, and pretty badly sometimes. But you might also "get it". Since you're free, and you're naturally built as a soul to evolve, you're going to "get it" naturally anyway, whether in this lifetime or another.

So I am not your master, not your boss, nor any such thing. I don't oversee some sort of sect. A sect is a group where the master is always right. The sect holds "the truth", and the individuals in that sect have been chosen by God. If the master is always right, it means that you don't have free will. This is a scam. A master cannot tell you the truth since it's an experience. A true master can only stimulate states of being in you, but you're the one who will attain enlightenment. This is something you will have to experience alone.

Many Forms but a Single Nature

If someone tells you that he or she holds the truth, please know that this is also crap. The concept of *Chosen* goes totally against Oneness. There cannot be separation. We're all souls evolving at our own rate and pace through manifested physical forms. This is why I say that if you have money to pay when coming to my seminar, or participating in an event online, you should do so to allow me to earn a living and pay my fees. Otherwise I would have to get a regular job because I have a family to care for, and I couldn't keep traveling the world giving those seminars. But, I have never refused access to my seminars to anybody who genuinely couldn't afford it, but who was truly commited to the wisdom   One's spiritual evolution must not be limited by one's level of wealth.

Why do I have this approach? Because I manage my teachings like in a temple, not like as a business. In a temple, if you have nothing to give, you don't. If you do have something to give, then it is wise to give as this is what allows the temple to work   Nowadays, the label *temple* is often different than the traditional *temple* most think of. In our modern societies, a temple can often have the function, the shape, and the form of a plane ticket, a hotel room, and a conference room that I rent for two days before going to another seminar in another country or back home. Or it can take the form of a computer, and people from all over the world attending at once. There was a time when people went to the master in the temple, and now it's the master who goes to the people. In fact, as you may guess, the way in which this all happens is irrelevant. It's a karma in our countries and culture to proceed in this way, and I surely will not fight it.

This is also why, when I give weekend long seminars, I always try to make Fridays accessible to anybody, for free. If you find that you have appreciated it, you should help me pay my bills and my hotel fee. If you find that you could've learned the same thing and have the same experiences you had in my seminars by simply reading a book, then please don't give a single penny. You need to go back to your books, because you're free, and I'm not attached to this wealth. I am not attached to money. My life is dedicated to spiritual evolution, not wealth. When I manifest, I don't focus on manifesting wealth, even if I have the power to do so.

Wealth does follow, but it is a "by-product" so to speak, much in the same way as the old alchemists did, turning their back on wealth so that they could then learn how to create gold. The universe is a bit like a young child. If you run after a kid, it will run away. But if you turn your back on the child, very soon he's going to turn and go your way, even run after you. This is how nature works. Turn your back on money, while being sincerely and consciously grateful for everything you have, no matter how much you have, and more money will come.

If you want to manifest more money, I'll give you the technique. Here it is

"Thank You!"

That's it. Gratitude. "Thank you! I'm so happy for all I have! I eat, I have clothing, I have shelter, I'm in a safe situation. Thank you! I'm so happy to have all this, this is way beyond all of what I really need!" If you're in a state of happiness and feel sincere gratitude for having more than what you truly need, more than what you need comes, because this is the state of being that you're in.

But please, know the difference between a whim and a need. Know what you truly want so that you can focus on it, instead of what you think will get you there. It's like this guy who wanted a big car. By quizzing him, we can get to the root of what he truly wants, and believe me it has nothing to do with the big car. The conversation could go as follows:

"Why do you want a big car?"

"Because I want to be impressive."

"Oh, so you don't want a big car, you want to be impressive. But why do you want to be impressive?"

" Well, because I want people to notice me."

"Oh, so you don't want to be impressive, you want to be noticed. But why?"

"Well... because I'm not just any nobody on the street. I want people to know I'm special."

And eventually, if you keep asking questions, you'll get to the core of the whole thing: unconsciously, that guy just wants to be loved, but he's so conditionned in his modern "needs" that he somehow believes the big car will get him there. So, this is what he's trying to achieve: unconsciously looking for love through a big car. Eventually, he'll find that the big car doesn't quite provide what he is truly looking for deep within. Not only that, but now he has to manage and care for the big car, payments, insurances, etc.

Another example, one that truly happened this time. There was that lady who came to one of my seminar on manifestation. She wanted to manifest a whole lot of money for herself. I told her that there was absolutely nothing wrong with that, but there must have been a reason why she wanted a lot of money. It was certainly not just to have a big number written on some paper or some computer screen. There was a deeper reason at the root of her wish. So I wasked her why she wanted to have a lot of money.

"Because I want to buy a house."

"Oh, so you don't want a lot of money, or at least, that's not your ultimate goal. What you truly want is a house, right?"

"Well, yes, that's right. But I'll still have to buy it!"

"I understand that, but you must know what you truly want to manifest, otherwise you may never manifest it! So you want a house, I suggest you to focus on that, and give up the control on how you think it must happen."

That was a novel idea for her. She had never thought about it that way. Then I asked her, "But why do you want a house?"

"Well, my husband and I plan on raising a family and..."
"Ah! Okay, so the true essence of what you want is to have a family, and the house is just so that you have a comfortable place to raise your family, isn't it? Why not focus on that? Focus on a family and a confortable place to live, and give up the control on how you want it to happen."

By focusing on money, while she wanted a house, and by focusing on a house while she wanted a family, she may never ever have manifested any of this, because what she asked for was not in line with her true desire. Maybe her desire would not be fulfilled the way she had planned, maybe the universe would not bring her a house to fulfill her true need. Being too precise on *how* it's supposed to happen may prevent nature to modulate and express the reality of what you truly wish.

At that point, the lady was beginning to really grasp how this whole manifestation thing worked. She was inquisitive and excited at the same time I asked her just one last question: Why did she want a comfortable environment for her family? Or, better yet, why did she want a family to begin with?

I was clearly not making her wish sound bad or anything, I was merely asking her if she truly knew why she had the initial wish in the very first place. It turns out that she did discover the real motivation herself. After having asked herself the right questions, the reason she wanted money was to experience love.

So now, she had gotten to the core of it. She didn't really care about the money, the house or the family. Those were simply ways or means which she thought would bring her the experience she was truly looking for. Deep down she wanted to experience love. So, I told her to focus on that, because the soul doesn't care about money, houses or kids. Love, however, is at the level of the soul.

Eventually, the lady did get a nice house to raise a happy family in. It didn't happen through lottery as she initially thought. She could experience what she wanted, although through slightly different means than anticipated. An old man had died, and the lady was on his testament. He gave her the house. In the end, the manifestation worked.

Our mind is so busy with so many concepts based on human intellectual and rational understanding, and most people want the "magic" to happen. Mind over matter, or so the saying goes. Well, it has nothing to do with mind, but everything to do with state of being. It is your soul, which is beyond logic and beyong nature as you see, hear, touch, smell, and taste it. It is your soul that has what is referred to as supernatural abilities- not your mind. Your mind is just a tool that you can use to synthesize or trigger a state of being. So use it, wisely, but don't think it's the only thing at work. Use it to visualize happy faces. Use it to get yourself in a happy state of being. And have faith. But, understand that it will not bring about what you want all by itself.

As you can see, there's a driving force behind all this, but you won't be able to tap into it if you just read, and read, and read even the best spiritual books out there. You won't be able to until you sit and practice and observe.

What State do You Live In?

As we've seen earlier in this book, there's happiness, there's suffering, and you need to go through both consciously. Only then can you become truly agile at synthesizing and remaining, in a given state of being, and then push them out in the manifested world. This is how the soul does it. In fact, this is what it has been doing from the very start. And you are that soul, you only have to free yourself from your inner clogs and attachments in order to let it express itself freely.

If you deny something, the true state of being that you're unconsciously creating is that there's something you don't want to see... so something happens to prevent you from seeing, sometimes even preventing you from seeing physically, like dimming eyesight. If you refuse to observe and feel abandonment, things will happen to force you into it, and you'll begin to be more and more alone. Your soul just takes what you already are within and projects it outside. That's how it works. If you're not conscious of what you hold within, things will seemingly happen randomly in your life. Ever notice how some people always seem to be in some sort of trouble, sometimes dragging on the same problematic situation for years and years? Is it truly a coincidence? Why do you think some people constantly struggle financially, some others always ending up in violent relationships, others get sick all the time?

I encourage you to become a master at creating states of being and existing as those states of being, freed from the blocks and the chains and everything that keeps you in your emotional dungeon. Nobody can do it for you. Nobody will save you. You have to do it yourself. Nobody will ever come and suffer for you. You also have to do it yourself.

Well, let me bring up a nuance here: a few very rare dudes can suffer for you, but they're crazy dudes. There's been this guy named Jesus, whom most people think said, "I came to take the sins of the world on my shoulders." But that's not what the original saying was. What Jesus actually said was, "I came to suffer the experience of others." He said it in his native language, Aramean, in such a way that it was later translated, for better or worse, as *sin*. Some confusion arose in the translation somewhere along the way, but basically Jesus did not say he was going to save anyone. He only said he was going to help us carry our cross (suffering) through his consciousness.

But 500 years before that, the Buddha said that he came to alleviate the sufferings of the world, not *save your soul*. How does he alleviate suffering? He looks at you, focuses on you, observes you. He pays attention to your suffering, and the suffering begins to dissolve. The Buddha has experienced suffering himself, so if you call his intention, he will look at you, observe your suffering. But you better not count on this: do it yourself.

You, yourself, pay attention to your own suffering and dissolve it. Consciousness applied to suffering dissolves it. When invoking some exterior power, you don't learn to do it yourself. You don't become better at doing it yourself, you don't become a master at resolving your own issues, so eventually it will have to be done all over again. You need the lesson, might as well do it yourself. You see, your soul doesn't mind suffering, it's your human that does. Your human definition, your perceived identity, your mind, your heart and your body don't want to suffer, but your soul doesn't care about this. Your soul thinks more along the lines of, "I wonder what this experience tastes like. Oh! This is suffering! Okay, what else now? I wonder what this other experience tastes like. Oh, this is happiness!"

It's like a child who's takes a handful of sand and shoves it in his mouth. Sometimes this single experience is not enough to bring wisdom, so the kid takes a second handful and eats it too. Until it hurts when the whole thing comes out at the other end. Whether it's a broken heart or a bleeding butthole, suffering brings wisdom and wisdom enlightens you. My example may sound a little juvenile, but it's really how it works.

If all this is a little abstract for you, here's a little inner speech you may want to try on yourself to see if it doesn't clarify things a bit. Ask yourself how you observe the world. Ask yourself how you perceive reality. From what perspective do you observe what seems to be a cause of suffering and what seems to be a cause of happiness? Ponder on this, and truly take the time to feel what comes up, without interfering. Do not rationalize: Feel. If you don't feel, you're not going anywhere, you might as well just keep dulling your mind with your usual activities.

On the other hand, if you only feel and get stuck there, you'll go nowhere either. You need to become a master yourself. Notice I didn't say "control yourself", but "master yourself". (We'll talk about control shortly.) Think, observe, feel, walk, experience. Try out things, experiment, have fun within this existence, discovering what is happy and what is not happy. Have fun experimenting it all.

This is playing with life, with existence. All of that will bring you wisdom. What we talked about so far has triggerred experiences and states of being in you. You felt it, you breathed into it, and now it makes a bit more sense. Just keep going. Even if you put this book down and never think about spirituality again in your life, you'll still be one step beyond where you were before reading the book, because of this little chat we had. Because of it, your soul has had a new experience, and it makes more sense to your human self. The experience is even more powerful during a live seminar.

From now on, each of your sufferings could be just a bit easier, or a lot easier. It's up to you. The fact that you took the time earlier in this book to think of some past situations when you denied and tried to push experiences away, and truly let yourself sink into the feeling, you now understand why denying and running away just hurts more and more in the end. We tried this little exercsie where we simply accepted the uncomfortable feeling, paid attention to it consciously and felt that it gradually lost power. After a few minutes, it still was not really comfortable, but it wasn't that bad anymore either. And then we learned how to fill ourselves with joy, consciously, not letting the natural forces to fill whatever void was left by the dissolution of one particular suffering,

This is what I call comfortable suffering. Willingly going to that uncomfortable place, without dramatizing it, nor supporting it with your stories, nor trying to fight it or be saved from it. Just looking at it. Understanding it. Becoming conscious. "Oh, I'm attached to something. . Oh, I'm afraid to lose it. If I don't detach from it now, eventually this thing will go away, or I will go away. I'm going to die someday. In any case, I'll have to detach..."

All of what we've covered so far will make more and more sense the more you observe it, think about it, look at it, feel it. Actually, all this is the cornerstone of existence. You don't even have to believe anything. All you need to do is to simply contemplate and experience. Some people will try to become happy by doing their best not to feel anything, denying, hiding and running away. Then, after a heart attack or an intense challenge in their life, they'll begin to think that maybe there is something to this whole thing about feeling emotions. If someone is in denial, it's because the person *does* feel something, otherwise there would be no need to deny in the first place.

I'm not a Christian. I'm not a Hindu. I'm not a Buddhist either. All those things don't exist anyway. However, I have studied those wisdoms. I got to the point of being ordained as a catholic priest. I eventually moved on leaving this behind. I also have been ordained as an Acharya, in a buddhist lineage, and I have also moved on, for the most part.

Then again, some people need such structures, systems and labels, so, when I speak to those people, I use those labels. They're great marketing aids. It's cool being that freaky Buddhist guy, or that freaky Christian guy. It gets people talking. It is part of my karma in this life to handle some of those things. If someone comes to me and wants to speak about Jesus, well, I'm in love with Jesus. And I'm in love with the Budha. And Krishna. And Vishnu. And I'm not being manipulative, or deceitful. I truly do love those teachers and their wisdom. The Buddha himself said that buddhism should be adapted in order to deliver it's teachings in the most efficient way possible according to the time and place it is being taught.

Notice I didn't mention the Koran, and this doesn't mean the Koran is bad.

It just means I have no competence in the Koran. If I pretended to have any, *then* I would be manipulative and deceitful. But the reality is that I have no competence in it. However, one thing I know for sure: there are holy men in Islam. I met one, and he was englightened. So there is some great wisdom in there as well. Of course, there are also a few freaks who kill in the name of their religion, but those are not only found in the Muslim faith. They are found wherever there are humans, regardless of what spiritual path they have adopted, because humans are still doing research. It has nothing to do with their religion. But then there's also karma which comes into play, and all that cause and effect concept.

Up until not so long ago (and maybe even still today), Christians burned their saints on pillars. It's so easy to bitch and judge other people when the only sample of existence is your limited lifespan, and whatever few situations you have happened to witness. I remember seeing my own daughter burn on a pillar 500 years ago, in front of me. Through deep observation and truly feeling it, there's a point where we realize that it's just a new experience. Let s try to make it happy. Do your best to be happy. No matter what you do, take the time to be happy for no reason. Smile. Breathe, and smile...

As a sidenote: those who enjoy the happy-facing technique and who like mantras: the word "Sukhi" means happy in Sanskrit. The word "Ananda" means bliss. The word 'Ram" is pleasure. So "Sukhi Ananda Ram" means

"Happy Blissful Pleasure". That's the mantra of the happy face technique we talked about. It's appropriate to recite it when you visualize everything as happiness, with happy faces all around and all over. Just overwhelm yourself with happiness. Breathe slowly and deeply while repeating "Sukhi Ananda Ram" every few seconds.

You don't like mantras? Don't do it. You like mantras? Do it. It will simply get results faster. It's a technique, not a law. We have no rules in our lineage. We have suggestions. And if you don't follow our suggestions, well... what can I do? We frankly don't care: everybody is totally free. We don't care because we found something that we could call blissful indifference.

Indifference is a blessing for those who are indifferent. For those who aren't indifferent, quite a few may tell me, "You don't care about me!" Well... exactly, you're right! I'm so happy, and it doesn't have anything to do with you, him, the economy, the weather or anything else! You should try it and stop trying to get others to care about you! Be happy for no reason! Enlighten already. Come on!

Seriously now, blissful indifference is just a state. It's not lack of compassion and it's certainly not disrespect. Indifference is not allowing the outside to affect the inside. It doesn't truly mean not to care, even if it sometimes may look like this on the surface. Blissfull indifference is not irresponsibility. It's gaining your power back. Take what you have outside and bring it inside.

It hurts your feelings when someone calls you a pig or treats you like a piece of crap. You feel bad and it hurts. But, now you have the tools to truly understand the hurt. Naturally, because you paid attention and acknolwedged the suffering of allowing other people to treat you like crap, you'll stop being affected when others, in their own mind, think they're treating you like crap. It won't matter to you anymore.

If someone gives me a gift, I'm happy. If someone throws a brick at me, I'm still happy! It has nothing to do with the gift or the brick. Of course, I'll enjoy the gift and try to dodge the brick, because, well, I may be enlightened and appear weird on the surface to some people sometimes, but I'm not stupid.

Don't Try to Help People
(Unless They're Ready)

Disclaimer: The following chapter is a very important one. It will provide information that will be of immense help in your integration process. What I am about to give you is a comprehensive grid of how the ego is built, or works. The grid is divided in seven main "compartments" each with three "variations", effectively mapping 21 masks of the ego, which I have labelled the Ego Road Map. While nothing is as clear-cut as what is presented below in real life, it provides a very good starting point to help you integrate your life experiences.

I urge you to please keep this new information to yourself: without the previous wisdom contained in this book, or without having been at one of the seminars I give, what you are about to read could do more harm than good to those you give it to, maybe even slowing down their own evolution. The logical and rational mind, once it has seen an information, usually closes the door to further investigation and wisdom. "Oh, I know all about that already. I've seen it all." For the mind, it's end of story.

If only the logical surface of the wisdom is understood, it may very well prevent the person from effectively *EXPERIENCING* the wisdom. As I have mentioned time and time again in this book so far: truth and evolution are not about facts but about experience.

Your Passion, Your Mastery, Your Evolution

I will tell you the same thing I always tell all of my students and disciples: Please, make your own decisions. Feel your own need to evolve, and let that drive you. Never start to believe that because you're studying with me that you absolutely need to go fast or do all the processes and all the meditation, etc. You're free.

In seminars, I always give a lot of techniques, but nobody is forced to do anything. I don't want to do pressure marketing to prove to you that you have to do any of it. If you don't have the passion to do it on your own, don't do it. But if you do want to become a master and be happier, then by all means do the practices, the meditations, the mantras. But it's all up to you.

The approach I have is very different from many spiritual classes and gatherings that I've seen or attended, where the group hangs together and everybody is encouraging, sometimes pressuring, other members of the group to come to the gatherings. They have this attitude so that the master, guru, or teacher can have as many students as possible. Everybody is pressuring everybody else and if someone does not show up at meetings, he or she is often put down and sometimes downright rejected.

As far as I am concerned, this approach is faulty on many levels. I always tell people who study with me or come to my seminars that if one day they don't feel like coming, then they should not come. And if they want to stop being guided by me altogether, then that is fine as well. Everyone should have the right to make their own decisions.

What I want are students that are solely driven by passion and that the only reason they study with me or come to my seminars is because they want it. Period. There is no marketing scheme, no pressure from spouse or friends, and certainly not from me. There is only the feeling of "I really want to be there.", which should belong to them and them only. Actually, I have even seen cases when some people had to actually fight to come to an event. In some occasions, a certain degree of passion is indeed required simply to rearrange one's life and obligations and to go through various degrees of trials in order to be able to make it and attend a seminar (whether it be through a live online seminar, or in person).

This entrains you in passion. Passion will be what allows you to become a master. Your own master. This passion, and only this passion, has to be your motivation. And those who know me will tell you: I do use my students' and disciples' passion as a teaching tool.

If you've been studying with me for a while now, and you see that someone who usually is present at a seminar doesn't show up once, or a few times, don't judge them. And yourself, if for any reason you cannot come, make peace with it. Passion is certainly not guilt, and if you happen to feel guilty, please by all means resolve this issue. You do not owe me anything, and I don't think any lesser of you for this. And remember what we spoke of earlier: if you don't come to a seminar, you didn't screw up.

Usually, as you progress, it will take you more passion to be in the presence of increasignly higher wisdom. In some instances, it takes a bit (or a lot!) of humility for people who study with me to simply accept the teachings that I provide since for the most part it's different than what they are used to or that they were expecting. There are concepts that are not always fun to contemplate at times.

I was conversing with someone the other day. That person was telling me how something in her life had disturbed her, and that such a thing should not happen. Then she wanted to make a point that it's normal to be angry or sad when faced with a difficulty. To which I replied that yes, it's normal to react that way, but it's also normal not to be enlightened, and it's normal to suffer.

But then again, some people want to stay normal and they especially don't want to get rid of some of their suffering (even if it doesn't seem to make sense). For some people, their suffering is dear to them, whether for the attention they get from others because of it, as a tool to manipulate others, or whatever other reason. This is their choice, and it has to be respected.

On the other hand, some other people don't want to remain normal. To those, I suggest: "Try this mind set. Try this approach. Try this way of thinking. Try that technique." Sometimes this disturbs some people, and they have to resolve it. Some other times, people embrace the advice wholeheartedly. In any case, there is always an experience stemming from all this, which requires conscious observation to be truly grasped.

Suppose someone spits on the sidewalk, and the sight is not pretty. Actually, it's enough to disturb you and gross you out. Instead of arguing that someone should not spit on the sidewalk, although this is debatable, you might want to bring your attention to the fact that it *does* disgust you, and that you might want to resolve the issue within you so that never again can something like this get to you. Arguing has never resolved anything: just look at the history of mankind. Arguing can be taken very far, to the point of death penalty and such other extremes. However, changing oneself from within has always been the most expedient way to go to alleviate suffering, especially of the person willing to do it.

So, getting back to that green spit on the sidewalk: any type of biological fear you may have, do your best to resolve it. Begin small if you wish and then build up on that, but if you don't do it, green goo on the sidewalk (among other things) will always have power over you. Another example: If you hate walking barefoot in a lake because the bottom of the lake is muddy and gooey, go there and feel it. Don't hurt yourself, but face it. Go through these experiences that demonstrate to you how much power nature has over you. If you're afraid of blood, go to a blood clinic to give some, and pay attention to what goes on within you when the needles pierces your skin and the blood drips out. Be conscious of everything and integrate.

Of course, it's not very wise to do stupid things which will end up hurting yourself either, but don't be afraid to disturb yourself in a manageable way and observe your reactions consciously as a teaching tool. If you can self-provoke fears that are not hindering you nor hurting you, and you have that passion and will to truly observe yourself and free yourself once and for all. Do it.

If you're afraid of speed, don't race your car to 100 miles an hour in a little country road so that you can face your fear. You might actually kill yourself, so of course don't do things like this. Try a roller-coaster that is certified to be safe instead. Choose safe options to challenge yourself. Even great masters don't play with life and death, but they do find ways to safely face what is disturbing them.

I'll give an example that actually happened to me. I was moving furniture around in my living room, and behind a desk was a big dead bug on it's back. This thing was huge, much bigger than what I was used to seeing. My first gut reaction was to step back. A bug is associated with dirt and creepiness. It triggers the fear of death, of decomposing. Bugs feed off that. So yeah, I had that initial reflex to move away, but I decided to face it: face my fear of dying, decomposing, rotting, and whatever else that dead insect triggered in me. So I picked it up, brought it very close to my eyes and looked at it. I put it on my arm, and looked. And I observed whatever surfaced in me until I was through with the experience. Then I threw the bug away.

Another example: there was a time when I was afraid of very strong winds in elevated places. So I forced myself to go on the top of a mountain on a windy day. I didn't go to the very edge of a cliff trying to prove myself that I could conquer my fear. The wind was indeed strong, it could have tipped me over and the fall would've been fatal. My ego could have found a way to stop what I was forcing it into. My ego didn't want to face this at all, and since I was forcing it to, it might have thought that killing myself was a viable option not to deal with the fear.

It's like extreme sports. Some people enjoy extreme sports that provide a huge thrill, but that are actually very safe with all sorts of safety paddings, belts and straps, etc. This is cool, but jumping stark naked in an acid-filled pool full of razor blades and guarded by german shepherds and mentally ill snipers to discover your biological fears is not wise. You need to find an in between: a threshold of acceptable risk and safety.

Because of all this, it is nice to understand the true range of what being free means. Most of the time, life brings you trials anyways, you don't absolutely need to always push yourself into them. You push yourself into them when you want to go faster, but this is not mandatory.

There is also a series of mantras that will accelerate your evolution. What those mantras do is that they force into your life everything that you have inside that isn't resolved yet. Then, if you're conscious, you can see all kinds of stuff happening that you can then integrate, but your life goes to hell. Before you begin to think that it would be nice to have those mantras so that you can evolve faster, I never record nor print them. Those kind of mantras are powerful enough to require extra caution when teaching them and reciting them, and only do this in person. And then, I don't teach them to anyone who asks either. Just knowing about them, without even reciting them, can have an effect which, if you're not prepared, can screw up quite a few things in your life.

Earlier in my life, I was taught those mantras, and I was told to recite them only from time to time. So in the beggining, I would recite them for a minute or two and everything was fine. Stuff did happen, and it wasn't always pleasant (it rarely was in fact), but I was conscious and I processed everything. Overall, the technique worked well.

Then I decided I was tough enough and I started to do the mantras for a half hour everyday. The result? I literally walked in hell. Almost everything that could have gone wrong did go wrong, all at once. Having to stay awake for an entire week, with a single 7 hour nap midway through the week, and resolve everything that comes your way is something I've experienced. Two periods of 72 hours of wakefulness back to back is not something your nervous system really appreciates. Those are times when you need to sustain yourself on soul, or else even more things will go wrong. So this is the kind of mantra that you may wish to do some day, but only when you get to that point in your training.

There's one of my very advanced disciples and teacher who wanted to go through accelerated evolution, so we sat together one day and I taught him the mantras. I told him to recite them for one minute daily, but he started to do them for a half hour. His life went to hell within a week. Don't do those techniques until you are ready. But, like I spoke about earlier, you can accelerate your evolution simply by wanting it, by giving yourself unpleasant challenges.

Usually, when stuff comes to you in life, it comes in little waves. If you integrate those little waves, you'll never have to suffer the bigger issues. It is when you don't want to deal with these little waves, because you're in denial and you don't even want to acknowledge them that the waves become stronger, energy builds up and sooner or later a tsunami wipes you off your feet. I suggest you to do what you can to avoid that.

So, what prevents you from integrating your issues? Our ego has a lot to do with it, although it is not the enemy that many make it to be. We can "map out" the ego and divide it in 7 major components, which in turn can each be divided in 3 ways. Of course, nothing is as clear cut as a sterile 7 X 3 grid in life, so please remain flexible when you use the information that I am about to share with you, but it is a good place to start.

Ladies and gentlemen, please discover the Ego Road Map.

The Ego Road Map

THE 3 DENIALS: FEAR, SHAME, PRIDE

We have ego reflexes that we unconsciously use to avoid paying attention to what makes us suffer in life. I call those reflexes "denials", and there are 3 of them: Fear, Shame and Pride. Those built-in "softwares" are blessings. They have ensured our survival for quite some time, but they're also what prevent you from becoming enlightened. It's like a beta version of a software: unrefined, still containing bugs and errors, etc.

Denials are what will make you not want to look at the next wave of suffering coming towards you. Eventually, the waves become bigger and bigger, and as counterproductive as it may seem, our natural instinct is to become better and better at denial. Some very, very proud people will even let their lives become such a mess when they get washed away by huge titanic waves. Others who are greatly ashamed always suffer great consequences stemming from their great shame. Some other people are very afraid and develop nervous system tics and habits, like locking their doors 3 times, constantly washing their hands, and such. In extreme cases, psychotic and sociopath behaviors develop.

So, fear, shame, and pride are the 3 denials of the ego. But denial of what exactly, you may ask? Well, usually when we deny something, it's not the thing itself that we don't want to see, but rather the emotion that it triggers, and we unconsciously use fear, shame or pride (and sometimes a form of a combination of those) in order to deny those uncomfortable emotions.

Just as for denials, emotions also come in a trio.

THE 3 EMOTIONS: ABANDONMENT, REJECTION, GUILT

Abandonment is when we have the impression that something left, or when we ourselves leave. Rejection is more the result of combined "push-pull" force: I am pushed away, or it is me who pushes away. For example, disgust is a form of rejection. When you're disgusted about something or someone's behavior- whether because the action downright grosses you out or you think it totally lacks moral values- you tend to push it away, to reject it. The same thing happens when you disgust someone else and they push you away. Whether you are the one rejecting, or the one being rejected, rejection is felt because it has nothing to do with who's doing it. It is the total experience, the emotion as a whole, regardless of who or what is involved.

The same thing applies to abandonment. If you abandon someone, you will feel abandonment. Guilt is a little easier to spot and recognize. Rejection feels full, abandonment feels empty. Rejection is like a positive (not positive as in "desirable" but positive in the mathematical sense) emotional pressure, which creates some sort of "overflow" pushing things away; while abandonment is like a negative emotional pressure which creates a vacuum.

Suppose you feel lonely, and you begin to contemplate it. When you do realize that you are feeling lonely, your initial urge may be to deny it with pride, shame or fear. This is when you need to catch yourself in denial and not flee from that feeling of being alone: sink in there. Stay in that feeling of loneliness until you become conscious of everything that feels lonely within you.

Eventually, when you accept it, you'll still feel the loneliness, but there will be no more suffering about it. But to get to that point you must bypass the denial and stay in this loneliness until it loses it's intensity. It's not particularly fun to do, but it's better to go through it for a short while and stop suffering about it than to carry it in you 24/7 and have it randomly hinder your happiness.

After you have consciously sat in this feeling and its grip has loosened up, breathe in and fill yourself up with joy. It's very important that you don't try to fill yourself up while the feeling of abandonment is not resolved, because you'll fill the void with anything and you may very well end up worse off afterwards. One thing at a time: feel the abandonment, sink into it and resolve it. Then, and only then, do some happy-facing like we discussed earlier in this book.

To cover up those emotions, the human ego plays a role.

THE 3 ROLES: VICTIM, SAVIOR, PERSECUTOR

I won't give much information here about these 3 roles. They are not as obvious as we would think. They are complex enough to have an experimental seminar only on the topic, and today we wish to go on with the entire ego map. So, we will move onwards.

The role of the savior is when you try to help someone out of a desire to attract attention and stimulate a false sense of importance to the victim. It is wonderful to want to help others. Observe yourself to see if you are helping out of compassion, or out of a desire to augment your feeling of importance, or give yourself credit. Regardless of your reasons, it is always good to help others.

The victim is the role we play when we are seeking the attention of a savior. It is often useful to receive the help of others, and it is essential to communicate to others our need of their support, when we feel we need it. Thus, do not prevent yourself from seeking help. Simply observe yourself, and see if you are honestly trying to resolve a situation, or if you will remain in your distress so you can keep asking saviors to give you attention.

A persecutor is someone who creates or supports suffering in other people's experience. Even more, a persecutor can pick himself as a target, and we become self-persecutors. If you observe long enough, you will see. Let us move on.

To operate in these roles, you use certain tools…

THE 3 TOOLS: POWER, CONTROL, MANIPULATION

Some people try to get something done using power. When that doesn't work, the person will often try to use control. If that still doesn't work, then the person will try to manipulate.

Sometimes, women try to overpower males, and often of course, it doesn't work. In general, a man will resort to power (physical force and violence) to have his way. So, what do women do then? They try to control the guy telling him what to do, etc. Most of the time, this still doesn't work. This is one of the reason why women become good at manipulating.

Power works most of the time for powerful men, so you have men addicted to power. Weaker men are addicted to control, and only a few men are really good at manipulation. Everybody manipulates, but only a few men are good at it, whereas women are almost ALL good at it. Of course, nature wants it this way, which ensures the survival of women.

Think of a recent situation when you used power, control, or manipulation in the last year or so. Take the time to think about it. Did you do this because you were playing the role of the victim, because you wanted to be a savior, or because you wanted to persecute? Was it to avoid feeling abandonment, rejection or guilt? Find it, go feel it. What is the emotion? The three emotions usually play some sort of role to varying degrees, but one stands out more than the two others. How did you not see it at the moment it happened? Was it because of pride, shame, or fear? What prevented you from seeing it at the time, and why do you see it now?

Through each of the seven ego components, your own ego will find it's way. It may have an attachment to this thing, so it will develop this need, which will manifest an expectation (an expectation that the need will be met) using a tool and play a role to produce an emotion which it denies.

Sometimes you're stuck with an emotion and you don't know where it comes from, and the denial, the role, etc. All seem blurry. So start from the emotion: is it abandonment, rejection or guilt? From there, try to determine which state you are in, which denial you are using (fear, shame, or pride). And then, with those two components identified, try to find out what role you're playing: victim, savior or persecutor? Then ask yourself what tools you are using: control, manipulation, or power? Then (and this is our next stop on the map), ask yourself what expectation are you trying to fulfill?

THE 3 EXPECTATIONS:
FALSE HOPE, OVERCERTAINTY, EGOCENTRISM

False hope is "I hope he loves me." You have an expectation that someone else loves you. "I hope everything will be fine." This is also an expectation. There is a difference between the state of being of someone being prudent, and the state of being of someone having a false hope (although the two are very easily confused, especially for someone in denial!). Being prudent is doing what you can to make sure everything goes fine. Having a false hope is tainted with fear that something may go wrong, but you hope it won't. The experience of those two states is very different, even if they look the same on the surface.

When having a false hope, you're fighting, you're afraid something will go wrong, so you push more false hope into it trying to convince yourself everything will be okay. You build up even more expectations. Those are the cases when if something indeed doesn't work out, the person will most of the time snap and even destroy the whole thing (objects, plans, etc.) simply because the inflated expectations have caused so much deception. This is very, very common in love relationships.

Overcertainty is taking something for granted. "I was sure this was mine."

Egocentrism is a little different. Egocentrism is not even caring whether it's yours or not. You just take it even if you know that something is not yours. It's a fantasy that you convince yourself is true.

"I was certain that my parents loved me!" It's normal to expect that your parents love you. But some people sometimes find out the hard way that no matter how strong their expectation, their parents still don't care about them. I know that it is perfectly natural and normal to expect your parents to love you. I also know that expectation brings suffering when they are not met! So, like I often reply to people who tell me that something is "normal": of course it's normal to expect, and it's also normal to suffer! And people wonder why I am so weird sometimes, why I am not quite "normal". Let me tell you: accepting to come across as abnormal is very little price to pay for true happiness. I am not complaining at all in this tradeoff.

That being said, I'm not stupid. I know it is very difficult for someone who's been rejected by his or her parents to pick himself off the ground and say, "I give up. I will mourn my expectation and accept that I wasn't meant to be loved by my parents." But the reality of it is that nobody who has ever been born was meant to be loved by their parents. It's just that most of the time it happens, so it becomes a norm (a normal norm, to be redundent). Thus, people have long ago taken it for granted and now it's part of almost any culture, of any period, in the history of mankind.

But no matter how much you take it for granted, the reality is that you were just meant to be born and live. That's it. Everything else is drama and expectation. So yes it's very hard when you find out that your lover doesn't love you, but it's not your lover's responsibility to love you: it is your own. If he or she does love you, well then great! Just enjoy it, but it's not something you can take for granted.

Those affective and emotional issues are the strongest expectations we have. Everything in you will say, 'He/She *has* to be in love with me. *He/She is my lover!*'

But I tell you: "No, he/she doesn't have to love you! You can keep your expectations and you can keep suffering when he/she leaves if you want."

You can reply, "Well, I don't want to be with a lover who doesn't love me! I'm not going to be with someone who doesn't love me!" I totally agree. And, one very simple solution is to leave the relationship and find someone who does. And when you do find someone who seems to love you according to all the hints that you have- be it because he/she told you, or acts a certain way, or you just have the feeling that he/she does love you, whatever *proves* it to you- then you'll feel safe to become his/her lover also, and this is what you want. This is all *okay*.

But what I am saying is: still don't have an expectation. Enjoy it while it seems to be true, most of the time it is. But using those kinds of arguments and trying to find the *perfect match* is still a way for people not to look at their suffering and to say that they don't want to find that love within themselves, wanting others to give it to them.

Of course it's fun to have a lover who loves you. Still, find a way to love yourself. After that, if and when love does come from the outside, consider it an extra, a bonus. See it as a side dish. Enjoy it. Just don't expect it, even if your ego is totally convinced that it's okay to have expectations. Again, my answer to this is that yes it's okay to have expectations, and it's okay to suffer.

THE 3 NEEDS: ACQUIRE, ACCUMULATE, ATTAIN

The three needs of the ego may be the part of the ego road map that confuses people the most as the distinction between the three is sometimes subtle. Acquire is when something is not mine and I want it, so I make it mine. Accumulate is more, more, more, more... Attain is when you set yourself a limit to reach.

You know those people who just accumulate stuff? For example, they already have enough plastic jars to put their food in but they still need to buy more and have their cabinet filled with all these 50 year old plastic jars that the covers don't even fit anymore because they're worn out or broken?

Why do we have those needs? What are we so attached to that needs to be fulfilled?

THE 3 ATTACHMENTS: PHYSICAL, EMOTIONAL, MENTAL

Attachments are pretty straightforward and self-explanatory, although their interpretation requires one to be able to identify them well. Let's use an example. Let's take someone who smokes. What kind of attachement could it be? Most people would say that it's a physical attachment, and it may be, but not necessarily. Smoking can stem from an emotional attachment if it's to be part of a gang. This other person might smoke because it has a certain look or matches a certain role, in which case the attachment is mental. This other person may be addicted to nicotine, in which case then the attachment is indeed physical.

Let's use another example, a guy who plays video games all the time, to the point where he's addicted and cannot stop. It could be any type of attachment, so it's hard to draw a line that applies to all. It's case by case. Is it a physical attachment because he loves the hormonal rush he gets while playing? Or is it rather an emotional issue, because he has his buddies online while playing and it gives him a sense of cummunity? Is the attachment mental, keeping his mind busy so that he doesn't have the time to think about how much suffering he holds inside?

When we first begin to identify our ego patterns, we quickly have the reflex of pointing a finger and saying: "It's this type of attachment, or that type of attachment." At first, identification can be as swift as erroneous. Over time, someone gets more and more agile with it and can spot subtleties more easily. The more we do it, the more we are able to sort out subtleties and eventually, we can decipher tendencies even in the most blurry situations.

We have an attachment, which produces a need for which we'll build an expectation. To meet this expectation we'll use a tool while we play a role that builds an emotional mass which we deny. In every pattern, behavior, reaction, reflex, etc. we do all that to varying degrees.

On the Road: Using the Map

This is the ego roadmap. However, if you want this tool to really help you and to use it effectively, and as I have mentioned numerous times earlier in this book, you must first learn to feel your emotions. You first and foremost need to learn to integrate, otherwise all that information will be useless. Your ego will simply pull all of your sensible strings to convince you that you must keep your expectations.

But if you do have even just a little experience with feeling and integrating your emotions, the ego road map will be of immense help and it will be much easier to do, and much more effective as well. You'll know more clearly what a deception feels like. A deception is an attachment that forces itself out, but you're still attached. Deception is the tension on the string which attaches you to the object of your attachment.

Pain comes when you're expecting something because you're attached to it, and that thing is not there, or it's denied to you. The tension of the pull on the string is what hurts. If you let go, if you cut the string, the pain will dissolve. All you need to do is feel the emotion, recognize how you deny it, check the various components of the ego road map we've just discussed. Of course written this way it sounds quite simple, but you now know that it requires being conscious and, most importantly, facing the pain.

In some situations, especially at first, use the road map to identify the seven components and three modes of the ego. But, as soon as you have a little bit of experience with integration using the ego road map, try to use it less and less. Don't lock yourself in a position where this tool becomes like a crutch. This is not the goal of the exercise. As I often say, when you have crossed the river, ditch the boat. When you become more agile and subtle in your integration process, just feel the emotion and sort out the pattern on your own. Eventually, you'll instinctively know what the denial was, what kind of attachment it was, what role you played, etc. You don't always have to cover and identify all seven aspects.

On the other hand, don't fool yourself by recognising only 3 aspects and then thinking your job is done. If you do that, the situation will come again, the suffering will come back, leaving you to think that the road map is bogus. This is why I urge people to experience instead of merely learning intellectually. So please do use the road map, do your best to identify everything that you usually try to avoid seeing until you are trained enough to do it on your own, but not before that. If you use only your intuition before you are actually well trained in this process, you will also be very intuitive at avoiding the full process.

If you sit in a suffering, consciously observing it without intention (not wishing it to go away, not wishing to transform it, but simply observing it without intervening), it will dissolve. Find an attachment and find out what need it feeds. You have an expectation built on that. What force are you ready to apply, and in which way: control, power or manipulation? Through this, are you playing the victim, the savior, or the persecutor? Do you feel abandoned, rejected, or guilty? Are you avoiding looking at it because of shame, fear, or pride?

All this sounds like a logic game and it can be if you only apply the information in the same sterile manner it has been written above. I can explain in words what the steps are, but I cannot explain to you how to feel the process. And, you need to feel if this is to have any kind of success. Sometimes one of these component will be fuzzy. It doesn't matter. Move on. As I mentioned earlier, nothing is quite as clear-cut as a 21 compartment grid. But the more you play with it the more refined your perception will be.

It may happen that you find that there is more than one role, more than one emotion, etc. This is okay. In fact, it is bound to happen more often than not. I divided each of the seven components into three variations, but each component suffices unto itself. For example, there is only one emotion, but it can be observed from three broader angles. So, from which angle are you looking at the emotion: the abandonment angle, the rejection angle or the guilt angle?

It's too subtle for an untrained person to just go into an emotion and naturally detect what "flavor" it has, so we put labels on it to help in the process, which will make it easier for the ego to get to the bottom of things. So instead of just saying "I feel bad!", putting a label on it (abandonment, rejection, or guilt) helps to refine the identification process.

As I mentionned earlier, the ego is a very, very cunning part of yourself, and if you truly happen to spot one of it's masks, the ego may resort to better, even more subtle illusions to make you believe that you're on the right path. For example, an ego can easily fake humility and compassion. It can fake being right about something, and it often persecutes if confronted.

It will fake humility by being shameful and playing the victim. It will fake compassion by trying to be a savior. It may be because you want to attract attention. You may play the savior's role because you have an expectation, etc. Whatever you can notice, start from there. If you notice you're playing the savior, start with this component, then work your way through the whole map, again. It is not rare that when you identify one layer, there can be one or more "deeper" layers which will also require attention.

For example, suppose a woman is in an apparently normal relationship with a man, and everything seems to be going well. She may still play the role of the savior, so she might manipulate because she feels abandonment. But why is there a feeling of abandonment? After all, the guy is right there and has never hinted that he wanted to leave the relationship. So, by looking a little deeper into it, the woman in question realizes that she only *fears* being abandoned! So there, she has her denial and her emotion. So she will manipulate and play the savior so that the person she "saves" will feel dependant, reinforcing the need to stay in the relationship (or so she thinks). So that woman has to ask herself, what does she expect, based on what need, and what is it attached to? See how it can be done? There's no clear-cut way to do it. Play around with it. This is just an example.

This ego road map simply gives you a workable system, some mechanical parts, to help you wrap your mind around them. It's like a kata in martial arts. You go through the figures, the positions and the movements. You practice in your mind and on the dojo mat until you get to the point where it all just flows naturally. And with further practice, it all becomes so much second nature that you can be in a real fighting situation and you will just go with the flow. The exact same principle applies to what we are trying to do here: with time you will be able to literally process and integrate stuff as it is happening without having to feel like crap for 2 days, 2 weeks or 2 months before being able to free yourself from it. However, as you may guess, this is a process and doesn't happen overnight. But the more you do it, the better you become.

The speed at which it will happen is mainly a matter of how much passion you put into it.

So practice with the structure, step by step, in order to master the 21 masks of the ego, learning to navigate your way through and around all of it's trails, to the point where you can process one emotion within a breath or two instead of half an hour. It basically is a way to train yourself in the ability to face any possible situation in your life as efficiently as possible.

Once you're trained with all this, one component at a time, one step at a time, practicing the entire roadmap for every experience you go through will be natural for you. Eventually, not only will you be better with the various steps of the process, but you will also be able to manage many steps all at the same time. For example, the denial, the emotion and the role can be obvious immediately.

At any given moment when you experience a situation, you will naturally feel: He left me... I feel abandoned... I play the victim... etc. Bam bam bam: your egos' pattern will simply reveal itself at once, instead of bit by bit. However, remember that many of your patterns (most of them actually) have been reinforced over many, many years, and it's normal not to be able to see it all at once at first. This is how the mind works, it's a mental pattern, but don't just *think* about it in your mind: *Feel* it in your gut. Feel your thought. Feel your ego, instead of just thinking about them.

Initially, you will find yourself relying heavily on the structure and may think lowly of yourself for being so rational. Please don't feel bad (too much) about this. It's normal to first go about it in a rational, logical way. You may feel an abandonment, and then study your grid to rationalize that it's a victim game, and so on. However, as you have filled all the appropriate boxes in your ego road map chart, you may wonder why the heck is it still hurting! Of course you'll still be hurting. It's still there. See, identifying the pattern and it's component was wise, but you still have to sink into it until it returns to consciousness. Don't beat yourself up if at first you have to think rationally at every step of this process. Just be conscious that thinking alone is not what makes this technique efficient.

Eventually, you will clearly identify one pattern, one entire scheme of the ego: the emotion, the role, all those components, checking your chart, your grid, or your thought process, double checking everything. But, if you did it only mentally, you haven't done much good to yourself. I know. I sound redundant, but this is of utmost importance if you want to increase your happiness and speed up your evolution. You *will* have to sit there, conscious of your control, of your attachments, of the tools you use and the roles you play. You will have to sit there and be conscious of all that, suffering it while it dissolves. But it will dissolve.

Consciousness is the solvent that dissolves, so mentally identifying the pattern is not sufficient to dissolve it. I, myself, still identify some attachments that I have and I also have to sit in them and observe them for them to go away. We have a tendency to just cling on to our attachments and never give that a second thought.

And sometimes you truly did your homework, you observed consciously, you sat in the suffering and observed it. And then you completely filled yourself with happy faces and envisioned your whole being, on every level, as one big *happy being*. You truly thought you were done, but then, the next day, you come to realize that you still have something there... not everything has quite gone away yet.

This is normal and natural: keep at it. Dig up some more. Go deeper. Keep practicing and refining your skills. Like I said, some of the patterns you hold have been densified for many years, so it's normal that some residue may remain, despite your best intentions and efforts. In many cases your ego has had it's way for almost all your life. Give yourself time. You have to spend quite a bit of time on one pattern in order to dissolve it completely. But once you have truly dissolved a pattern, you will have dissolved it for every instance in your life when you played by your ego's rules.

The good thing is that even though it is not instantaneous, this kind of conscious work on yourself is roughly 10 times more efficient than if you had let nature do it's thing. So suppose you have learned to be a very good victim over the course of the last five years. Six months of conscious observation will suffice to dissolve it completely.

Sometimes you'll even be able to connect events in your life, including those that happened many years apart. You may remember something that happened when you were four years old and realize that it looks and feels very much like the pattern you witnessed yesterday. Different people, different setting, but exactly the same type of experience.

I'll use myself as an example. True story: I was four and it had to do with me not getting a candy, then later I was 17 and it had to do with me not getting intimate with a girl. I was 21 and it had to do with me not being able to afford something to eat... Different people, different setting, same experience. Because I hadn't resolved the candy issue when I was four, and because I hadn't resolved the sexual issue when I was 17, the whole thing simply grew in intensity until it got to the point where it was not just a whim anymore, but my survival itself was at stake.

So I did sit in this suffering, starved, thinking of other times when the same pattern arose. Some memories will come back to you and some won't, but whatever comes to you, I encourage you to process it so that those at least are out of the way. And then, you may have identified and processed everything and still suffer, because of the amount of consciousness that you put in this experience to build it up, so you will have to apply the same amount of conscisousness to dissolve it.

You see, some of the patterns you will indentify have been reinforced by you over and over for years, and in many cases over many lifetimes, without you realising it. But don't bother yourself with this at this moment, take care of your life here, now. Take care of whatever you remember as far as you can remember. When those are dissolved properly, everything will be dissolved from your experience.

It's just that you have to take the time to sit in the emotion and tell yourself, for example: "I really feel guilt." Just be aware that your mind will probably try to interfere and thoughts may pop up in your mind like: 'Well, I know there's no reason to feel guilty! It wasn't my fault! I'm a good guy!' Since going through an integration process like that is not always fun, your mind is going to try to convince you of how good you are and how it's not your fault in an effort to take the pressure off. But no matter what your mind says, regardless of all the good reasons and logic and rational arguments you can have, you will still feel the guilt. You can tell yourself, 'I did the right thing. I know I did the right thing, but she told me I was an asshole, and I still feel guilty.' This is why I'm telling you not to think about it, but to feel it. It has nothing to do with reason or logic.

Guilt doesn't depend on whether you did something bad or not. You only have to think that you did something bad and it won't fail- you will feel guilty. Expert manipulators and those good at playing the victim know this very well, unconsciously if not consciously. If someone suggests to you that what you did might indeed be bad, then a part of you which is afraid that it might indeed be bad will trigger the guilt naturally. Heck, someone could blame you for something you haven't even done and despite all your logic, you'd still feel hints of guilt! Oh, and by the way, do you recognize the denial here? Do you notice the fear, from that part of you which is afraid?

This has happened to all of us. Remember when that happened to you? Someone blames you for something you didn't do or for something that doesn't even concern you and the guilt comes? Guilt does't need you to do something bad to rise. It only needs your doubt.

While I'm on that subject, I'll emphasize on the trap I just exposed: Suppose you feel guilt. You may very well rationalize, 'No! I don't have to feel this guilt. It's not my fault! I don't have to integrate anything or feel this guilt. It's not my fault!' Well, it doesn't matter if you are responsible or not. The guilt is there. If you don't go feel it, you'll just keep suffering it anyway. It's not your fault, but you still feel the guilt and suffer. So you need to calm your mind which tries to stay in denial, and take your ego off it's auto-pilot mode, both of which are just trying to *justify* the experience and remove pressure instead of letting you integrate it.

Emotional Integration

Emotional integration is the process of taking something that is outside and bringing it inside. It's not re-integration, because it was never inside you to begin with. You're just obeying the forces of nature which planned things this way. The moment something happens, most humans will try to push it outside by condemning, finding someone or something else to blame, etc. "It was his fault, not mine! I have nothing to do with this! I'm not guilty!" (Well, maybe you're not guilty, but you sure do feel the guilt!)

Then, once the initial intensity of the emotion wears off and you objectively take a look at your reaction, you think a bit more about it and come to realize that, 'Okay, yes, maybe it was not his fault, but it certainly was his *responsibility*! He's the one who screwed up! But, I still feel the guilt. Okay, I let go. I'll integrate it. I'll just bring it back in anyway, even if I don't have anything to do with it.' This last sentence is the point you want to reach if you are genuine about your aspirations to free yourself and be happy no matter what.

To integrate, you need to breathe slowly and deeply, you need to be present in yourself, inhabiting yourself, and accept whatever discomfort that rises up. You let yourself be swamped by the emotion. Let it invade you while all you do is look at it and sit in it. Allow yourself to just be completely conscious of it, feeling it, and observing it until there is nothing more to observe, nothing more to feel, nothing more to inhabit, breathing is natural and you're still conscious.

After this, there will be a figurative "hole", some sort of void inside of you, a kind of emptiness. After a period of emotional integration, you need to fill yourself up again, with happiness, just like we have covered earlier in the book. I teach this every time I teach integration. After every integration session, put smiles and happiness and consciousness into every part of yourself, and pay special attention to that part of you inside that you feel is now empty. Otherwise, you'll let the natural forces fill the void for you the way they want, which may be good or may be bad, it may be happiness or it may be suffering. In any case, if you don't fill yourself back up with hapiness on purpose, the "refilling" mode won't be under your control and you may end up pouring in more garbage than you just dissolved. First, integrate what you have to integrate, and then get into a happy mind state. Defeat the ego that doesn't care about bliss and would much rather reinforce separation than happiness in you.

Some of you may begin to think that I am repeating myself over and over and that this book could have been half as long and still deliver. Let me tell you a little secret. No matter how often I repeat this, no matter how I insist on this, I predict something for you: In not so long, you'll integrate tons of stuff, and right after a session of integration, even if I warned you numerous times about it, you will not do the full process. You will not fill yourself with happiness and smileys and joyful thoughts. Once your integration is done, one day you'll just get up with that huge void in you, that huge empty space just begging to be filled. You'll just flip the channels on TV, watch what's on the news (which is crap for the most part), check your emails, read the paper, eat something, etc. You'll just *forget* about putting happiness back into you.

Then after a year or two, some of you will write to me, or come to one of my seminars and tell me, "Maha, I did integration for such and such a time, but I still don't feel the bliss." To which I'll probably ask if you really did it with your consciousness or if you only managed it at the mental level. I may ask if you really felt or if you rationalized everything using your ego road map grid for months. And if you did really feel for as long as it took, did you make sure to pour happiness back into you before everyday life and natural forces had their way by filling you with whatever random garbage your ego may think is perfect to keep you chained to the bottom of the dungeon, blocked from the experience of happiness? Did all your integration sessions end as great and joyful events as they should?

After a given period of integration, you may feel that the emotion is still going strong. If this is so, keep feeling it. However, if you keep feeling, keep feeling, keep feeling, but don't go further in the process by identifying the ego pattern that triggered the emotion, not only will the emotion stay there, but it's going to come back stronger later on. I did mention many, many times so far in this book that feeling an emotion is the very first thing you need to do otherwise you're wasting your time. Well, if it's the first thing you need to do, it goes without saying that it's not the only thing you need to do: it's only the first. The most important one, yes, but only the first nonetheless. If you don't identify the attachment, you don't identify how you deny the emotion, the role you play, the tool you use, etc., what you are trying to dissolve will not dissolve.

Sometimes, you can just feel an emotion and it does go away... for a short while. This may lure you into thinking that you're truly done. In some rare cases, it may be so. But usually, if you haven't identified and then dissolved the ego behavior also (the pattern, the animal genetic code that urges you to go, for example, kick the neighbor's butt instead of being responsible), the whole "pain producing machinery" is still in place within you, doing it's job as it is supposed to. So, you will eventually behave again in the same way and reproduce the emotion yet again. You may have dissolved it the first time, but you haven't removed the tools you used to create it in the first place, which was misperception, a misunderstanding of reality. So the technique is not at fault here. Everything is in perfect working order. What needs to be adressed is not the technique, but your understanding and your application of it.

The misinterpretation or misunderstanding of reality will sound like: "She left me." or "He went away.' or "He called me a pig and I'm insulted!" or "My parents are dead." etc. The right perception is: "It was never mine to begin with." "I am self-contained." "I have no real identity. I only believe I have one." "I have everything that I need inside of me." "Nothing can hurt me." "Well, if nothing can hurt me, why does it hurt? Let's find out." Now, *this* is a good perception! This is the inner dialogue you need to entertain as often and as consciously as possible.

Most trials in life have to do with desire, especially emotional and physical desire. We have the need to survive, which in our modern and rich societies is about one percent of our trials. Once your survival is secured, there's another one percent or so of insignificant trials such as: "He called me a moron! He said I was stupid! He cut in line in front of me!" That one percent mainly has to do with a hurt pride, not exclusively, but largely. In any case, it's trivial. For example, when you want a promotion at work but you don't get it, etc. If your survival is not threatened, there's a good chance that it has to do with this insignificant one percent.

Then the remaining ninety-eight percent is related to your desires: when you were ashamed because you were caught naked once, or because you didn't perform sexually as much as the other wanted you to, or you had more drive than your partner and were left still hungry so to speak. Pride, shame, and fear related to sexuality. You can pick those for yourself. Find one such situation (yes, you have many of them) and try to find the denial, the tool, the role, the expectations, etc. For example if you're a woman, "Well, I expect to at least be able to bear a child!". Men don't have to look very far: you guys have plenty to deal with even if you picked only the sexual performance aspect.

But, before you can resolve experiences that deal with desires, you have to resolve your one percent of survival experiences. Pick a time when you were afraid not to eat the next day, when you were afraid of being killed, or beaten. When you were afraid of an accident. All those experiences that you are still carrying around within you and that are running in the background like a software, unnoticeably, on your computer. Then, you can deal with the one percent of insignificant stuff; and then, after that, the desire trials of the remaining ninety-eight percent.

Seriously, Don't Help People
(Unless They're Ready)

A word of caution: I briefly mentioned it earlier in the book, but let me emphasize it again. Unless someone can understand all of the wisdom of the ego road map explained earlier, I advise against using it. So don't go around trying to teach it to other people to help them, even if it's been a lifesaver for you, and even if you have the best of intentions. You may very well hinder them way more than you could ever imagine.

Just as I've been telling you all along, and just as I repeat, repeat, repeat over, and over again in live seminars: The first thing someone has to learn is to feel an emotion. That's it. It's the very, very first basic step that has to be taken and on which ALL the others will be stacked on. Feel the abandonment, rejection, or guilt: the three emotions we talked about. That's sufficient to begin with.

You'll see that even at this very basic stage, saying to some people, "Feel the emotion inside you..." will be more than enough confrontation for them to react. Of course, you'll understand that their reaction is based on either fear, shame or pride. In other words, they're in denial, but please don't confront them with that. Feeling an emotion is the first step, dealing with denials is the second. So if this first basic step of feeling the emotion (abandonment, rejection, or guilt) doesn't go through, and if they are in denial with fear, shame or pride, I urge you to **stop** immediatly. Don't try to provide further wisdom. ***Just Stop***. Why?

Because you're going to ruin parts of their life and they'll start to hate you sooner or later. Their ego will wise up and begin to actively create and build any and every possible defense mechanism that it can come up with against whatever wisdom you tried to force upon them. And they will associate this wisdom to you, because you have keys that would lead them to evolve, and this is the last thing that their ego wants. So they'll create and rationalize reasons to hate you.

So I urge you to please satisfy yourself in teaching someone just to feel an emotion. You'll hear some of them really make a first step forward. They may tell you, "I did! I felt the emotion real good, and I kept feeling it, and don't ask me why or how, but it eventually was so much easier to bare!"

Now, you'll know perfectly well that this hasn't resolved anything, but at least two very important things will have happened. First, they will have freed themselves from that emotion for that moment, and they feel that freedom. This is excellent because now they know how such freedom and lightness feels. So keep encouraging them in that process. The second very good thing that will have happened is that now they will be open to at least consider looking at their denials, which would have been impossible before in almost all cases.

Now, I'm talking about you trying to teach those people close to you. Of course some people will read this book, or view my videos, and if they hate me, they'll just put the book down or turn the video off. I don't mind if someone hates me. But don't ruin your own social environment even if your motives are good, even if you truly want to help someone, unless you're ready to deal with what may result.

Another thing you may want to check within yourself if your urge to help others is bugging you this much: your own savior pattern based on pride. "I'll show you how to free yourself from suffering! I know how to do it. I've done it, and I can get you out of your suffering! Hear me out..." and you begin teaching to the cute barmaid behind the bar, while the only thing she wants is for you to pay for your drink, give her a hefty tip, and to buzz off.

Most people who learn about what is in this book, who practice it even just a bit and who reap the rewards usually tell to those close to them: "I have the key to evolution! I know how to resolve any type of problem! I can free myself of any ego situation, and I want you to be free too!" Let me tell you this: It's none of your business! Detach. Don't expect others to want to do this. Don't expect others to want to stop suffering. They may pretend they don't want to suffer, but a lot of them unconsciously love it.

As a matter of fact, even if you do this integration process quite often and are very dedicated, don't even expect yourself to be that inclined to evolve. You'll see what I mean when you start digging the deeper stuff and realize that there are parts of you that you still don't want to see, despite the best of intentions. Now, imagine someone who is not even yet open to the idea...

I'll say it again: to really help someone, go one step at a time and don't skip important ones. First, teach them to feel the emotion. When they don't react adversely to this, show them another step, which would be the denials. Those will be the hardest to sink in, but if the person doesn't react to that, then you can begin to slowly talk about other components. Give them this book, or show them one of my videos about the ego road map. Or, better yet, encourage them to participate in a live event on the web, or to come to one of my seminars in person.

The moment you go beyond emotions and denials and you're starting to talk about roles for example, and you're really starting to pick into their dark little secrets, many people will retreat and close themselves shut like an oyster. Even if they'd never admit it if their life depended on it, their inner dialogue will go something like, 'Oh, no. He saw my ego! He spotted what I am trying so hard to hide!" Even if you think you know someone well, and have for a while, you may only know the surface. Most people have absolutely no idea of how cunning their own egos are. They just go along with it and believe in it without question.

Even you may not even be aware of ninety percent of your own defense reflexes. It's only when they pop-up and you happen to catch yourself that you'll go: "Ooooh! I just did this!" That is *if* you catch one of your own reactions. Very often, you won't. Among those who read this book, I have met many in person. Notice how you have reacted when, during one of our conversations, I did bring up one of your mechanism and reflex. As a side note, let me be clear: if it is not going to help you evolve, if you are not at a point in your evolution where you can hear what I see in you, I will never disclose it to you. My goal is not to ridicule anyone.

Sometimes it may take a while to identify a pattern, and even longer to dissolve it. But once you've truly integrated it, once you've really observed it, felt it, stayed in it consciously, you'll be done with it for life. You'll see that when you try to integrate an emotion, especially at first, your mind will try to distract you with interfering thoughts, and sometimes even physical discomfort (itchiness, pain in the legs, lower back fatigue, etc.) Keep at it. Don't hurt yourself, but don't give up at the first signs of distraction: this is exactly what your ego is trying to do because it feels that another little part of it is going to be identified and dissolved

Shame has a lot to do with guilt. Not all the time but often, shame is hiding guilt. Fear has to do most of the time with abandonment. Pride has a lot to do with rejection. And, so on. Those are not set in stone. They are tendencies. All patterns have tendencies towards one of the emotions, one of the roles, one of the denials, etc. But a good integration session is rarely that linear. There is often a mix and match of various components. It's all over the place. The more you do it, the more refined you become, and the more efficient the whole process is.

CONQUERING DRAMA

One day, I asked one of my advanced disciples and teacher to take care of setting up a little meditation and teaching mat for me. The one I still use up to this day in seminars. It was in between two teaching sessions and I had asked her to go to a store and buy something in order to do this, and I acted in such a way as to put pressure on her. So she went to the store. She bought a few other things she also needed at the time. So, she comes back to the seminar and realized that she had totally forgotten about what I asked her. She hadn't purchased what she needed to setup the mat, so she couldn't take care of it at that time.

Of course I had set her up somehow by putting pressure on her, and the plan worked, so I used that as a teaching aid. I asked her how she felt for having forgotten. I asked her if she felt like she had messed up somehow. I then asked to my student what she thought I felt towards her for having supposedly messed up? She said that it would be normal for me to be a little annoyed, maybe not angry nor mad, but a bit annoyed.

Now let me ask a question to you, the reader. I'm taking myself as an example here, so that you can apply the situation to yourself. If I see complete enlightenment, can I let an exterior cause annoy me? If I want to be thoroughly happy for no reason, no matter what the circumstances are, how well would I do if such an insignificant thing could disturb me?

Most people take for granted that, as a normal human being, I would have been annoyed since my student had not taken care of my meditation matt the way I asked her to. Maybe some masters with high expectations, or those who like to command others, or those who have power trips, maybe they would be annoyed. And I happen to know a few.

But I also know a few masters, including me, who don't see a meditation mat as a meditation mat. I don't see any of my students as having "messed up". Heck, if you ask me, I'll tell you that I don't even exist as I am perceived. I should not be a cause of guilt for you, nor anyone, no more than you were ever a source of annoyment and suffering for me. So I effectively used a real life event as a teaching tool, and I quizzed her and the others in attendance at the seminar who had witnessed the event about all of this. I asked them to go deeper within themselves to unroot some of their own ego mechanisms. After all that, I told my student, the one who had forgotten about the mat, that she could feel very good about herself, that she had never messed up to begin with.

Some other people sometimes write to me and tell me: "Oh, you must be so tired of getting my emails!" But how could I possibly be affected? If I don't want to read an email, all I have to do is press on a simple key: *delete*. To suggest in your emails that I would be annoyed of your presence is simply a lack of experience. People just don't realize how valuable they are to me. All my students are valuable. Truth be told, even if I've never met you, the reader, you are very valuable to me, and it has nothing to do with the fact that you bought this book or not. I know I spent a good part of this book saying that the concept of worth and value had to be dissolved, but I also have to use words to communicate, even if they are not always as accurate as the experience I wish to convey.

It is belief in the space-time continuum that prevents us from always being in contact as One. Although time and distance do not exist, my 5 senses and my rational mind certainly tell me that it does, and my soul tells me that I don't have the time to answer all of you. I often ask my students who write to me how they feel when they receive a reply two full weeks after they've written to me, and the reply they get is, "Thank you for your email. I'll read it soon.", and then never hear from me again about this? Now I ask you: how do you feel when you call a family member who doesn't care about you? In short, what I am asking you is how do you feel when you allow an exterior cause to put you in a state of being other than simple happiness?

We sometimes feel some form of detachment when people leave our environment (students leaving school, kids leaving the house, friends who go away, etc.) We must get into the mindset that kids, friends, parents, etc are not ours. There is love, and stuff just happens. That's it. End of the rationalization. There is nothing more to add. Everything else is drama. Things, people, and events come, last a while, and then vanish. Nothing is permanent, which is why we get annoyed when we want some things to remain a certain way. We want to stay happy, but we allow exterior causes to affect us.

For you to conquer drama whenever something affects you means that you have to look at it, and find a way to resolve it. But what is the first thing we do when something disturbs our inner state of peace? We attempt to control in hope of dominating life (good luck!). We could try that for years, but we'd eventually learn it doesn't work. We have those great metaphysicians, motivators, pseudo-spiritualists, New-Age fanatics, etc. who tell people that it is possible to have the power to create life the way we want, to have the power to manipulate things, to be in control. If someone believes this, it's simply because they don't know any better. Yet.

Control is ego; Mastery is Self. Control is outside; Mastery is inside. How can you develop self-mastery? You first have to let go of your denial the way we spoke about earlier. Once you have identified it, it's easier to let go afterwards. But again, don't learn to analyze. Learn to feel. If you keep it intellectual, you'll identify it, and then, your mind being satisfied, you'll just move on and keep clinging onto whatever you're trying to dissolve within you. This is why you need to feel. While it may require some kind of discipline at first, overtime you'll master this and you'll naturally identify and dissolve denials on the spot.

As a side note while we're at it, let me ask you the same question: Do you, the reader, sometimes feel like you have messed up? How do you feel about it now? How did you feel about it when it just happened? What was the feeling? How did you deny it? How did you find a way to not look into it at first? The denial was hiding an emotion: Abandonment, rejection, or guilt. Feel it. Everything else is drama, and drama is simply forgetting that you didn't screw up. How much do you allow exterior stuff to put you in states that you have not decided for yourself as an empowered being? Some people naturally have a good grasp of that, because they consciously choose what they allow to affect them, because of the fun of it.

Suppose a woman wants to make sure she is loved, and somehow screws up by current standards. Her screwing up is simply a sign of her incompetence, and she'll constantly find new ways to summon the attention of people in ways that they respond to, until she can find what she's looking for within her.

Don't pretend that you don't need to be loved and that all you have to do is to love everyone. If you can mourn the need to be loved, it means that you are already an almost fully realized buddha, and you would not need to be reading this book (or probably any book, for that matter). Don't play the game that you're done with all this. Don't pretend you're so evolved already.

New-Age hippies may try to do this, pretending that they're enlightened under their immense ponchos, driving their flower covered caravans. I have nothing against all this of course. Just don't let the surface influence you. And don't let your own surface influence you, either.

So in life, you're trying to be loved, and you think you screw up now and then, and screwing up makes you feel guilty because when you screw up, you fear that people won't love you. To make up for this, you play the role of the victim, the savior, or the persecutor, sometimes more than one simultaneously.

There are tons of things we could say about the ego, but the most basic thing is: What do I deny and based on what emotion? And then you must stop thinking that you screwed up! Let's just say that you acted in a way that is different than what others (and maybe yourself) expected, if you want to call it that, but anything other than this is pure invention. The only way to truly screw up would be to prevent yourself or someone from surviving. If you kill someone on purpose, then yes, that could be considered a major screw up, although from the Buddha's point of view, it would certainly not be. The Buddha would most likely say something along the lines of: "Oh, you killed the physical body of another being. You'll just pay karma for it. That's all. No drama." And life would go on.

If you did kill someone, maybe you allowed this person, because of his or her own karma, to be killed by you in order to go to a better existence. So maybe all is fine! But, you don't know that, and if you do kill someone, there will be sufficient evidence displayed by a large enough number of people to tell you that yes you did screw up, even though you maybe didn't.

If you threaten someone's survival, prevent them from eating, from physical safety, from being clothed, and from having shelter, then you're close enough to screwing up. Otherwise, it's just a fantasy that you did. Of course it's also wise not to do your best to cause suffering to others. Maybe stealing from someone, making fun of them on purpose and calling everybody names doesn't threaten anybody's survival, but it may not be the best way to go about in life either. Be compassionate.

Most of us at some point in our life have felt that we once screwed up at least one relationship. It could be the relationship with a lover, a child, a boss, a parent, etc. It doesn't matter. But I'm telling you again that, no, you didn't screw up. Thinking that you did is just a lack of understanding of how things work. You did research and development hoping to be loved, trying to find love outside of yourself, and you found out how incompetent you were at that. That's all.

But because of that event, you have an eye of judgement on you while you should rather have an eye of understanding. And by that, I don't mean an eye of pity. "Oh, poor you..." has never solved anything. That's not understanding. It's playing the victim-savior thing. By an eye of understanding, I mean something along the lines of, "What did I just do?! I want to understand it. Let me observe this as objectively as possible." Now, this holds the promise of the greatest evolution. Use compassion, not pity or judgement.

Suppose someone lies to you, and because of that you decide to end the relationship. Then, thinking back, you feel that you screwed up. You ended the relationship because someone lied to you, and you don't have compassion for that behavior. You believed in the drama. You played the along with the game and you believed in it. But let me ask you this: What in the world has changed if someone lies to you? How much money have you lost? How much air has run out of your car tires? Will you sleep on the same mattress you did the previous day? Has your house's value decreased? What has changed? No matter how someone else behaves or speaks, what changes?

If you cannot have a decent relationship with someone, you can end the relationship or find ways to be at peace with it. There's no need to go to war over that. Let me be clear on this: your ex lying to you did not have the power to affect you except for the power *you* gave him or her. You *wanted* to feel sad or mad for being lied to. You played the role of the victim on your own. "Yes, but she lied to me!" or "Yes, but he lied to me!" I understand that, but in the end... What changed? Your expectations, maybe, but what else? Some people will say that "something inside" changed, that the trust is gone, etc. Well, *trust* is really a socially acceptable and glorified way to mean that one has expectations. There's nothing more to trust than that.

Of course, it's hard to maintain a healthy relationship with someone who lies, depending on the lies. So you can choose to either be at peace with it if possible, or you can choose to end the relationship. There is no good or bad way to deal with it. If you choose to end the relationship, you don't have to work yourself up into this hyper-sensitive, offended state of being. All that reacting is going to do is nourish drama.

I'll repeat it again: There is no way to free yourself from those kind of emotions unless you learn to *feel*. Don't think about a situation: feel it. You are only doing research and development: gaining competence along the way. You weren't bad back then, and you're not bad right now.

When you can broaden your perception of life events, it's easy to appreciate people just stumbling their way through life, trying to learn how to love, just as it is easy to appreciate a cute little kid trying to stand up and take it's first baby steps. When you look at you with a judgmental eye, please remember to not require from yourself to be a master at running marathons right from the start. You must first find a way to stand up and not fall back down on your behind, and without anything to hold onto. Or rather, while trying to hold on to things that you think are stable (like your identity), but that never were, never are, and never will be.

At other times, you are aware that you are snapping. You are aware that you are losing it. And yet, you still let yourself loose. You see yourself poisoning your own life, and you sit back and watch the show, while the ego does it's thing with the puppet (that puppet would be you, by the way). You'll just go through the whole event as a by-stander, watching yourself become angry, do and say all kinds of stupid things and do nothing about it. Then, after a few days, problems arise as a consequence of not taking responsibility to master your own ego back when you could have, because you consciously and willingly didn't.

If you see that some huge emotional wave is coming, try having this inner dialogue: "Oh, I'm about to become angry. Whether I attack him and yell at him or whether I keep it inside and deal with it, there's going to be pain anyway, so I might as well handle this properly. I know anger is building up... What is it again? Oh yes: breathe... and feel... I'm in a state of pride... This is what's hurting inside. This is what angers me. I will not be proud about it. I will not step up and defend my rights, this is just an ego reaction, an ego that is afraid of losing it's place, but there is no place to be lost, and no place to be gained, except in my own mind. I'll let go. I know I'm not losing anything My survival is not threatened right now." *This* is mastery! *This* leads to efficient evolution!

It has nothing to do with control. Control is still wanting to destroy someone but refraining from it. Control is feeling the force of the urge to strike but applying the same force plus one percent to refrain yourself from doing it. *This* is control, and it hurts. Control is like sittng on a bomb hoping it doesn't hurt your butt too much when it goes off. Mastery is disengaging the bomb right at it's source.

In your daily life, your trials are almost never a threat to your survival They're just a threat to your pride and to your self-esteem. Just get rid of both. Dissolve the concept of pride, and dissolve the concept of self-esteem If you have low self esteem, then you need to build it up first. If you are already at the point where you do have self-esteem, then you need to dissolve it. Don't have self-esteem. Have Faith, instead.

Destroy the concept of value. If you destroy the concept that you need to be valuable, you will also stop feeling worthless. I'm not telling you to become worthless: I'm telling you to dissolve the concept of worth and worthlessness, and to discover the concept of non-worth. Don't build and then rely on self-esteem. Self-esteem is acceptable to operate in society. When you just want to be functional in regular society, pride and self-esteem are somewhat useful to accumulate money, to get recognition from others, to have a lot of goods, etc. It's useful to pretend being happy when in reality what you want is power and to be recognized and acknowledged by others.

But you can get rid of all that. Dissolve the idea that you need to establish yourself in society. Dissolve the value or insignificance you have in the eyes of others. Dissolve the need for approval you want to get from others. Dissolve the very concepts of approval and dissapproval. Dissolve the idea that you are separate from your environment... Dissolve... Dissolve...

Most of you are normal mammals figthing for your rights. Let's use an example where someone owes you some amount of money, and it doesn't appear that you will get it back. Of course, it may appear that you will lose a few dollars if you don't argue with that person in this situation. So please, do argue, get angry, and make your right recognized; and also please lose your inner peace, a few hairs, and a few hundred neurons in the process. "I don't want to lose money! I am going to fight! I want my rights to be recognized!" I understand all that, but is it worth losing your mind, your health, and your well-being over this? If you think so, please be my guest while I enjoy the show.

Some people will always fight like good capitalists who want to accumulate more, establish their rights, be loved, be approved, etc. This is all drama. This is all part of a theatrical play, which everybody cast in it believes.

I'll give you the key to conquer drama: Whatever you seek outside, find it inside. It's as simple as that. Now, please understand that this is a metaphor and try to deepen your understanding of it. Of course you can't find a Mercedez within you that you can pull out to drive, nor a playmate to marry, nor money to buy yourself a nice trip to Fiji. This is not what "finding within what you seek without" is all about.

What I am saying is that whatever experience you wish to have through the big car, the nice clothes, the cute hunk or hunkette, this experience can be found within. Whatever experience you wish to have by means of outside interaction can be found inside of you, in unlimited supply. So if you want to be loved, love yourself. Don't wait for a good reason to do it. Just do it, especially if it makes no sense!

You are creation of spirit, of supreme consciousness, how could you be anything else than marvelous? How could you not be a wonderful being? You've been created by what many call God. You are extraordinary. Love yourself just for that. If you're waiting for a good reason to love yourself, then there will also be a good reason to hate yourself. It means that you're still waiting for an exterior reason to validate your states of being. You don't need any permission to be happy. You don't need to get permission from a big paycheck, not a big house, nor the latest stereo system. You don't need approval of your friends, or the priest, or your boss. You only have to want it, and focus on it.

Many people tell me "But why I should I love myself?!", and I always reply this: "Because it will make you happy. Is this not a good enough reason?" If you dissolve the concept of self-worth and of worthlessness, you will stop thinking that you don't deserve to love yourself. The concept of deserving will also dissolve. You don't deserve to love yourself, nor do you deserve not to love yourself. Just do it anyway!

What do you do to prevent you from getting what you need from within yourself? The only thing you need from the outside is what your outside is made of: more or less organic matter that make up your shelter, your food, and your clothes. Survival stuff. That's it. Then, once those bases are covered, you may still like to have contact with people, then just go and have a regular social life. It's wise to do so! Just don't allow this interaction with other people prevent you from experiencing self-love.

When you get annoyed, you're giving them, or that (whatever is outside) the power to make you unhappy. This is not mastery. It's not worthlessness. It's not bad. It's merely innocent incompetence. But it's not mastery.

Again, when I say that the key to conquering drama is to find within you what you seek outside of you, I am talking about the experience and not the physical object. "I want my car out there! They stole it! I'm unhappy!" If your car gets stolen, you need to learn a few things.

First of all, it was not *your* car. It was *a* car. Dissolve the concept of possession, so that dispossession doesn't make you unhappy. Then, dissolve the concept that it was a car: it was not a car, although this is a bit far off for the purpose of this book. This is Zen teaching, which is not the point right now.

When we die, what do we learn? We learn three very simple things: First, we learn that our identity doesn't exist. Second, we learn that owning something doesn't exist. Finally, we learn that being in a relationship with

XYZ (person, object or concept) doesn't exist either.

Our identity is not something that we had at birth. We built it up as we went along. Suppose your name is Simon. When you die, your name is not Simon anymore. If you change your name to something else, you don't cease to exist. Thus you were never Simon. The label *Simon* is man-made and only refers to whatever you believe yourself to be. Your human identity that you forged over the years doesn't exist.

If someone were to insult me and if I stood up before that person saying, "Hey, you don't insult a master like me!", there are quite a few things I'd need to remind myself. First off, I would need to remember that I'm not a master. Then, I'd need to remember that the concept of master doesn't even exist. This concept is only possible when there's someone, like a "disciple", calling someone else a "master". Not only that, but it's not even because he truly is a disciple and I truly am master. It's only because of the type of experience he is having, which is defined in his mind by having someone (a master) and someone else (a disciple). The master and the disciple will both die, and when they do, neither will be master nor disciple, but soul without any identity.

If you think that you deserve to be paid for your good services that you provided for an organization and that this organization doesn't pay you, you can, out of wisdom and prudence, try to get the money that was supposed to be given to you as you expected. But will you allow it to make you unhappy if it doesn't happen? Stop believing you were doing something for that organization. You were not. It just seems that way.

If you think someone owes you something, be intelligent and ensure your survival, and try to get the resources that were supposed to be given to you. But, if it causes you great unhappiness, just forget that it was your money, and it disappears. If someone steals something from me, I'll just completely let it go. It was not mine anyway. I'm happy and because I let go without entertaining unhappy feelings, I relieve the other person of the karma, because he didn't steal something from me since I know consciouly that I never owned it. Only my conditioned human thinks so. Thus I free two people's karma at once.

Some people ask me how they can relieve someone else of his or her karma. The obvious answer is this: Oneness. There's only karma if there's a conscious trace of resistance such as "This is bad! He is bad! He stole from me and now I suffer!" However, the person who took something that is not his own (even if ownership is an illusion) still needs to know that it was not appropriate to lack respect for someone elses' illusion of property. In taking something that isn't his, instantly that person is setting himself up to learn some lesson. You don't have anything to do about this, except take care of your own experience and dissolve your own illusions. The person will have experiences that will remind them of the suffering they caused and that they will have to integrate their stuff some day. You don't have to apply justice yourself. Divine justice is perfect and never fails.

There was this guy who was in jail, for a theft he didn't commit, and there's this buddhist priest asking him how he felt about being in jail and not deserving it. The guy replied: "Hey hey, wait a minute before saying I didn't deserve it. I am actually paying for the other little thefts that I truly did without getting caught, some I may not even remember! It's cool. I'm happy with that. I'm at peace with it." What else is there to add to this pure wisdom. This is the kind of mindset that will free you from a ton of suffering.

You need to evolve your perception to get there, but first, you must realize that we usually react to painful situations with fear, shame, and/or pride, and it hides an emotion of abandonment, rejection, and/or guilt. Everything else is drama.

Whatever we seeking outside, we should seek inside, except for basic survival (and even that has been dissolved by very evolved master, but that's another story). It doesn't mean you have to give away all of your stuff, nor that you should not protect your belongings, but it does mean not to fight and resist against non-attachment when the lesson comes to you. Do not fight against letting go. You were born meant to survive and live happy. You were not meant to own stuff. You were not born with the concept of property. Yes, we do *own* things because it's cool, so play along since you were also born creator. But, you were not born with luggage. You didn't pull a canoe out of your mother's womb when you were born, and you won't bring a sofa with you when you die.

We spoke earlier about the concept of identity. Some people identify themselves so tightly with the various labels that make up their self-fabricated identity! "You don't piss off a Smith! Don't you spit on my mother's reputation like that! I'll show you if Canadians are wussies!" Come on! You really need to let go of pride and of the idea that your family's name and legacy, or any other label for that matter, stands strong. Stand strong by your own Self. Don't think your family, your country, your profession, or God knows what other intangible concept need any defending from you. You think you're Americans? You're going to die and be born in China to remind you that you're not. Let's go even broader: you think you're European? White? Or even human? You'll be born in Asia, or Black, or whatever else to remind you that identity is bogus. And I'm not even talking yet about coming into existence elsewhere than on our tiny little pebble we call Earth in this huge universe, but that's another story. The point is, let go of your identity. Just let go.

You prefer pistachio, chocolate, vanilla or strawberry? Well, those preferences are also part of your identity. You are not the body, you are not that thing which tastes. Yes, you have a body, and that body has the ability to taste, but remember that owning is just an illusory concept...

Stop reffering to yourself as your preferences. You may prefer techno music, and hate heavy metal. Of course, you can force yourself to listen to some heavy metal as a teaching tool. So you could play some heavy metal music, and pay attention to your reactions. Or not. It doesn't really matter. It's only a question of whether you are trying to free yourself or if you're still buying into the fact that you believe in what you convinced yourself was true.

If you ever chose to try that, just don't drive yourself mad by playing heavy metal for days on end, the volume turned up to the max in the name of evolution. Respect your limits. As I like to say, please suffer comfortably. But if someone plays power metal nearby, just disassociate from the belief that you hate that type of music. Realize that it's just a preference. It's part of your forged identity. Just throw it away and think to yourself: "Oh. Noise. Okay." After all, if you had to work a whole day in some loud environment, you wouldn't care as much, would you?

We often hear that there is good pride and bad pride. You can label it as good or bad depending on the situation if you like, but one thing remains: good pride causes suffering, and bad pride causes suffering. So whether it be good or bad, it will eventually cause suffering. The same applies to self-importance, self-esteem.

I'm not saying self-esteem is bad. In fact, you need self-esteem while you believe that you could be worthless. You need to build yourself a base concept of yourself, an identity that makes you worthy of something. Eventually, when you're ready to remember the whole of who you truly are, you may try to contemplate happiness simply as it is and tell yourself: "Okay, I will accept that I'm not the best in class. In fact, according to some scale, I can be considered the worst. But it's cool. I'm okay with it I'm at peace. I'll accept the fact that I'm the last one to get to the finish line, and that I'm the poorest, compared to those I am compared to. It doesn't really matter anyway because I'm just so happy, and I don't need a reason to be."

Being happy, without having any reason, is a key to happiness; but to truly conquer drama you need to go even beyond that. Go beyond the concept of your identity. Strive to become a saint. Whether you succeed or not is totally irrelevant. What is relevant is for you to shed the fear, shed the loneliness, shed the need to own things. Please don't misunderstand my words: I didn't say to get rid of your stuff, I said to get rid of the *need* to own stuff. This way, when your belongings leave your current experience, it will simply vanish without you suffering about it. However, while you do have those things, enjoy them! Make the most of them, appreciate them, have fun with them!

This is Budddha's teaching, the middle way. Not infatuated by exceessive luxury, but not suffering because you sorely lack the basics either. Be comfortable, no unhealthy excess, no unhealthy lack. Have stuff around you, enjoy it while it's there, and happily move on when it goes away. It's that simple.

Simply become conscious that clinging onto physical objects, people, or even intangible concepts such as titles, only serves one purpose: to make you suffer in the end. All those things that you so dearly hold on to and that you want to keep, tightly associated to your identity, is what eventually makes you unhappy.

However, like I said, please understand that owning something is not an automatic cause of suffering. It's not as straightforward as 1) I have a possession; therefore 2) I'm unhappy. What *is* an automatic cause of suffering however, is not letting go when detachment comes. You can own as many things as you want, but if you insist on keeping everything that way, then you are in fact trying to control the outside world. Eventually, the outside world will evolve in a different way than you think is desirable for you, and what you hold onto will go away. Nothing lasts forever. And as long as you want the outside to have an effect on you inside, you're setting yourself up for ache, tears, anger, and frustration. As long as you want your mate, your car, your job, your bank account to make you feel good, then you have to also accept that you want them to make you feel like crap.

Now, back to the story of my meditation mat I spoke of earlier. If I had allowed myself to believe that I could get pissed off about the fact that it was not properly set up by my student, I would be allowing something outside of me to affect me and cause me to become unhappy. So my student supposedly messed up my meditation mat, and I'm happy. If my student had not messed up my meditation mat, I would still be happy. My happiness has nothing to do with with what my student did! I just asked her to take care of it, and then I put pressure on her, made her stressed about it. I spoke fast and loud, giving her unclear instructions that only apeared clear in the heat of the moment, doing my best to confuse her on purpose so that there was a chance that she'd mess up. And, she did. She messed up mastefully well: she completely forgot about it! I never expected such an effect!

Some people will say that this is manipulation, and they're right. I'm not hiding that fact. But, there is one major difference in this case: I didn't do it to gain anything from anybody. My one and only goal was the evolution, not only of the student in question, but of all those who attended the seminar that weekend. Yes, I set her up, because we learn by experience. But, I have not threatened her survival, and I made a point to remind her that not only did she not mess up, but I was happy, and that she should be too! Not only that, but most important of all, we were in a comfortable setting, amongst other seekers who all knew each other and who would not judge what had happened, but who wanted to understand what was going on on a deeper, much deeper level. All in all, it benefited many.

There are masters out there who are extremely unattached, and you'll hear them tell you: "Just do whatever you want man. Life is like an acid trip. I don't care. There is Love and stuff happens. Be happy!" On the other hand, there are other masters who will indeed get all offended about the fact that someone is not a good disciple. And I don't mean playing the offended game as a teaching tool: I mean truly being offended.

But I ask you, what is this!? A *master* who gets offended? A *master* who thinks that a disciple exists? A *master* who thinks the disciple has *messed up*? Up to a certain point, this is nonsense! A disciple is not someone, it's an identity, which requires a relationship to another identity (a master) to exist. I'll repeat it again: get rid of your identity!

My disciples are not mine, and they're not disciples, and I'm not a master. It's fun to play the master-disciple game. It's cool, and it's useful to use those labels, so that our rational minds can take a break and make sense of it all. But please don't believe those inventions to be true. What is true is your experience, not the labels you put on it.

Now, let me throw you a curveball and switch all that around: How could you possibly affect someone else?   Unless you threaten someone else's survival, you were never the cause of someone elses' suffering.   I've been talking to you about all the things that affect you because you give those things the power to do so, and now I'm telling you that you could never possibly have affected someone else except for the power they gave you through their own incompetence in the search for love outside themselves.

So if you believe that you caused suffering to someone else and you cultivate the guilt of that, please realize that you're believing in the drama. The only thing you can do to cause them suffering is to threaten their survival, but they don't know that.   They will think that if you call them names, if you don't approve of them, if you laugh at them, etc. that you will be the cause of their suffering.   So play the game.   Respect them.   Don't go steal their TV thinking it doesn't belong to them anyway.   If you did so, please look at your own experience as well.   You would most probably be taking that TV because you wanted to own it.   Karma will do it's thing.   If you use your rational mind to play games on nature, nature will play games on you.

Do you sustain the belief that you have made someone else mad or sad?   If so, please look at this: summon back the emotion, feel it, breathe into it, and resolve it.   Get to the point where you are conscious that it's an illusion.   If you only think it's an illusion, you'll still feel the guilt.   this is why I emphasize so much on the importance of feeling experiences, instead of merely thinking about them. Each time you were incompetent in sharing the experience of love, you were not the cause of someone else's suffering. Their cause of suffering is their own non-enlightenment. That being said, I strongly encourage you to act with compassion.

Compassion is not indifference in the sense that you don't care. It's indifference in the sense that what triggers suffering is an illusion. The person may feel pain, but where tha pain comes from is the illusion. In this sense, indifference can be an experience where you are neither affected, nor do you want to affect. You're not putting energy into it to tip the scale in either direction.

Please don't confuse this with the simulation of indifference, which is plainly called arrogance. Arrogance is pushing something away because it disturbs you, pretending that you don't care. You do put energy in it. You pretend to be unaffected, but you are so affected that out of shame, fear or pride you put energy to block it off. There is pressure coming towards you, and you apply pressure to block it out. It's trying to control instead of trying to master. This is not authentic compassion. It's denial disguised as compassion.

Someone who is compassionate will have this kind of dialogue: "I'm so happy and I'll do my best to help you find happiness as well. But, if you are unhappy and you want to stay there, I'll respect that. I understand you are suffering. I wish I could help, but I hope you understand that I cannot do anything about it." This is the kind of inner dialogue that someone who is compassionate will entertain.

Someone who is arrogant will appear almost the same on the surface, but the inner dialogue will be quite different: "Don't pester me with your damn problem. It's none of my business. I walk head tall. I'm so not affected, so masterful." This is arrogance disguised as compassion, but it's built on pillars of drama. People who are arrogant are not happy, no matter how much effort they put in convincing you (or themselves) that they are.

If your wife, husband, kid, friend, boss, etc. is unhappy, there is nothing you really can do about it. However, you can care and be compassionnate. Just don't fall into the "savior" trap. See, there are two ways of caring for others: The compassionate way, guiding someone to find happiness with themselves; and there's the savior way, reinforcing the idea that happiness comes from outside (you) and hoping to get a lot of attention out of it. This is usually what people do when they try to prove to others (their wife, husband, friends, etc.) that they really love them, unknowingly hoping to puff up their own self-image in the process.

In any given population, there are always those who try to make everyone happy. If this is your case, please know that there is nothing wrong with that, but ask yourself what you get out of it. Do you feel important when you're helping others? Do you feel happy just making others happy? If you feel important, this is very good, it means that someday you'll look at your savior pattern who wants to feel important. If you pull out a more noble reason, such as making others happy makes you happy, it's good also. It means that someday you'll realize that you are still looking for happiness outside of you.

What is contained in the previous paragraph doesn't always go down well when I tell people about it. Some people often tell me: "Well, of course it makes me feel good to help my loved ones! I'm not going to help someone if it makes me feel bad!" I understand that, and I totally agree. It's wise not to force yourself through experiences that make you feel bad. However, the only thing I am saying is that if you help someone because it makes you feel good, you must also acept that some events will indeed happen which will make you feel bad. Why? Because you believe in the concept of worth, of self-importance.

Again, I am not saying that it is wrong. It's important for you to see this, but please understand that your experience still feeds off the concept of savior, of worth and of worthlessness. This person deserves your help and it makes you feel good to help him or her. This one doesn't deserve your help and it makes you feel bad to help him or her. Please see this.

I am not judging you nor condemning you, far from it. I am simply pointing out the fact that the ego is very cunning and will find a way to rationalize anything. And by the way, this also applies to me: I'm no different than you. I also catch my own ego play tricks on me from time to time, and I also have to observe myself and integrate. Now, you can take the wisdom, or reject it. To me, it makes no difference.

Let's suppose that you are very compassionate, and that you do your best to make someone else happy. Now, for whatever reason, let's suppose that not only is this person not happier because of your action, but she is downright angry. If you truly are compassionate, then you are compassionate for yourself as well. If your actions brush them the wrong way, you won't be affected. You were doing something for the greater good, but it didn't work. What else can you do? The other person may be mad, but you're still happy. Or, you may have succeeded, in which case the other person is happy, and you are also still happy. Your happiness has nothing to do with the other person's happiness anyway. In the eyes of most others who have never contemplated that kind of wisdom, you may come across as indifferent and not caring, while in reality this is not the case at all.

Don't try to feel super important, and don't feel super unimportant either.

Destroy the concept of importance. Find self-importance as Self, not as a human. Let go of pride and know yourself to be a wonderful being. Not a wonderful person with an identity, but a wonderful being without identity.

We saw that with the happy-facing technique, we can put ourselves in a state of happiness just by focusing on it. The same technique could be used to feel sorrow, anger, etc. You have made yourself cry in the past in order to attract someone else's attention at least once in your life, have you not? If not that, you have done other things to attract attention, like being angry for no really good reason so that people would acknowledge how important you are.

This shows that you are indeed the master of your emotional state. A lot of people spend hours a day observing and contemplating what they see as problems in their life, thus provoking that unhappy feeling in them. It never occured to them that they could try just the opposite: consciously contemplating the good things, the happy things, the blissful things. And I am not merely talking about *positive thinking*. I have already explained time and time again in this book that *thinking*, even if it is positive, is not sufficient. Instead of positive thinking, try positive *feeling* for a change. Do that for even just 5 minutes a day, and see if just that doesn't already make a huge difference.

You know now that you can put yourself in a happy state just by focusing on it. Simply removing the concept of comparison from your mind will dissolve a lot of issues already. Forget the idea that you are valuable, and forget the idea that you may not be valuable. Just put yourself in a state of being that makes you happy without anchoring it outside. Just close your eyes and feel yourself to be great, just for yourself. I'm not talking about the feeling of being great in the eyes of others: forget others. Think of yourself, alone, right now, just you, as a great person. Wonderful. Satisfied and happy, for no reason except for wanting it. You can put yourself in a state of happiness simply by will.

Please see that every petty state of dramatic emotion you've been in in your entire life was a simulation done exactly the same way. To conquer drama, you need to accept to be beyond your pride, beyond thinking your screwed up, beyond comparison with others. Everytime you feel that there is some drama going on, please understand that you are simulating it. I agree, sometimes the simulation looks very convincing, but it is still a simulation.

Some people sometimes perceive me as this sort of weird spiritual freak who is never challenged. But let me tell you, I can also be under pressure, I feel pain, and I cry just like anybody else. Granted I have done a lot of integration, and I am rather good at catching my ego on the spot most of the time, but there are times and situations where I am also challenged. It takes quite a bit, but it happens.

For example, after the very first seminar I gave in Amarillo, Texas, I waved people goodbye, waiting for everybody to leave. Nobody knew how I felt in fact, unless someone was very attuned to what is not picked up by regular senses. It was impossible to know how I felt. I didn't show any sign that I was suffering. I was smiling and joking and all, waiting for everybody to leave.

There were just a few helpers who are close to me who were still there, and they don't really care anyway. Then, when everybody else had left, I started to cry heavily, because that was the experience I was having at that time. I didn't begin to cry until anyone who could have reacted had left the room. I know a lot of people would have been all upset, caught into the drama of their own interpretation, some would have tried to help, some would have freaked out, some would have thought to themselves: "Oh my God! Oh no! Maha is crying. The master is in pain. Oh this is so bad!" Drama, drama! The reality was that I had played with natural forces during the whole seminar, and I was simply paying karma for it. Overall, I even had fun.

Now, look at yourself when you set up drama in your own life. Sometimes, you know that you're not feeling as sad as you'd like to show it, you're just not feeling very good, but if someone comes by, and you feel confident with them, then you really start the show. The tears, the bowed head, everything. It was not comfortable when you were alone, but now that soomeone with whom you feel comfortable is present, boy do you let yourself loose! Look at any kid, you'll understand what I mean. Kids are very good at this as most have already begun "learning" to use their ego, but they haven't learned all the social restrictions, yet. So, the kid is not feeling so great, but as soon as mommy walks in... WAAAAAAH! Notice how a very young baby will not do this. A very young kid will cry if it doesn't feel good, and stop crying when comforted. It has not yet learned to dramatize in order to get attention. But, that changes soon enough.

The worst part is when we we get to a point where we don't even need an audience anymore to create drama. I'm not talking about finding some time alone by yourself to consciously observe the suffering in order to dissolve it, I am talking about locking yourself away and then building up the drama, telling yourself stories and believing in them, just because you enjoy it. Please don't misunderstand me: not everybody does this. Some people have so much stuff built up within them that it can indeed be overwhelming at times. Those people need not be told they are acting childish and just making up drama, far from it. They need compassion, true compassion, as their level of suffering is way deeper than regular day-to-day drama that most people enjoy so much. But those kind of people are way fewer than you may think.

You have the power to stop drama, and many of you still want to play with it, only because you enjoy it, because it's fun, it adds spice to your life. It's cool to be so overwhelmed with joy and excitement, and that comes with being so overwhelmed with pain and sorrow. You haven't suffered enough drama yet, so you want more. Why even read this book and pretend you want to get rid of your suffering if you like it so much? Again, I'm not sayin it is the case for everybody, but it does apply to many more people than we think.

Want to hear another funny thing? Even though you are now aware of what goes on in your mind when drama occurs in your life, and even though you can stop most dramatic situations almost instantly, and even though you have the power to remain in a state of happiness, you will put this book down and in a couple of weeks, a couple of days or even a couple of hours, you'll discover how wonderfully incompetent you are at remaining in this state of bliss.

However, don't think I am judging you, and please don't judge yourself either. I am telling you, this is normal. Even if you know what to do, there is something called *conditionning*, which you've been subjected to for most of your life. To change, this is a process, and not just something you do once and it's over. Give yourself some time.

Suppose you engage in a conversation with your wife or husband in a couple of days. The conversation may grow into a discussion, and soon into an argument. You'll certainly be under the impression that there may be some drama there. As soon as you catch yourself slipping, force yourself out of it and into a state of happiness using the happy-facing technique.

Then ask yourself the basic questions, without denying your emotions "Why am I so proud? What am I defending? What is my standpoint, my position or my opinion when facing this person which I believe to be my partner? What am I trying to nourish through my identity as a spouse?" You may begin to think that he or she owes you at least some level of respect. If someone doesn't respect you, find a way to get rid of the concept of respect compassionately. Please see that your wife or husband is not necessarily supposed to respect you. Your lover is not born to respect you. They should, of course, as it contributes to pleasant communication and harmony, but that is not their main purpose. You, yourself, can respect your lover, your friends, your family, but that is not your main purpose either. Be conmpassionate Don't pester people just for the fun of it. Remember that while you know now that others aren't the true source of your suffering, they may indeed believe that you are the source of theirs. Don't make it a point to be disagreeable just because you know you can't screw up.

That being said, it's also a fact that sometimes, stuff happens. Sometimes you're not trying to be disrespectful. It may be an issue about two people aiming for the same thing for themselves. Two individuals believing that they have the same right.

There are tons of people on this planet fighting over tons of reasons, because of misinterpretations of the same issue. Sometimes it's not even a matter of who wants what anymore! Some people just don't want to lose. They don't want to be labeled as losers. Losers are not held in high regards in the eyes of others (see where this whole "self-esteem", whether high or low, ties in with this?), so some people fight just to win, battling their way through life and wondering now and then what the hell is missing from their life, wondering why they are not happy! It would be so easy to just stop the fighting and just let go.

It would be so easy to simply allow others to interpret your action as accepting loss while, in fact, you won't be losing. You will just be letting go of your own cause of suffering. Let them keep theirs if they want. If you do choose not to fight, don't allow the impression of failure to grow in you. Don't fall prey to your ego that will try to convince you that you failed to fight well, that you're less than the other person, unworthy. Don't let your ego, who's so right about everything, push you into a state of wanting to win an argument just for winning's sake.

Even if you are indeed right, how far off are you really if you're not happy? Many will argue that being right, and driving their point across *is* what makes them happy. How deluded. How enslaved to their ego. Let them be. There is nothing you can do for them. But as far as you are concerned, how about not caring if you're right, or if they're right? How about not caring if you win or lose, or if they win or lose? How about not caring about being approved or disapproved, how about not caring about proving anything? How about just telling yourself: 'They can believe whatever they want. I'm done with this. I'm going back to a state of happiness. Anyway, I'm not winning or losing this argument, regardless of what egos may think. It's not an argument anyway, it's just a cause of suffering.'

Suppose that someone owes you a thousand bucks and doesn't want to give it to you. In your ego's opinion, of course you have to battle your way to get it back. The fighting and arguing may not be a happy event, but you're not going to let this bastard get away with *your* thousand dollars, are you!? Hey, it's all good. If you want to go on that path, be my guest and go after the guy who owes you. What will happen once you get this thousand dollars back? Will you be happy? Yes, you may feel some form of satisfaction. After all, you won and he lost. You sure showed him not to mess with you! So yes, you are satisfied, but deep down, are you happy in the true sense of what happiness is? You spent a lot of energy, time, ressources and frustration in nourishing drama because to you, $1 000 was worth at least this much hassle for you.

Now, don't misunderstand me. I'm not saying to let anyone take from you, especially not your survival resources, in the name of "letting go". This would not be wise. If it only requires a little bit of energy to set things straight, a calm discussion, an agreement, an amicable arrangement, then by all means do so. If the only thing you have to do is to ask the person to give you back your money, and he agrees to give it back in a few installments, then it's all good.

But if you have to increase your chances of getting a cancer, if you end up shouting at your kids or wife because of the stress, if you have headaches, if it takes you forever to fall asleep at night because all you do is think about this moron who doesn't really understand compassion (no more than you do if you're hell bent on waging a war against him...) is it really worth it?

It is you who decides at which point you let go. There is no right or wrong, and there is no rule set in stone. There are only various choices which will bring about varying sets of consequences. You are the one who decides when and where you want to be happy, or if you prefer to keep spending time, thoughts and resources on not being happy. You are the one who decides how much stress and anger can be bought for a thousand dollars. From your own point of view, what is money's true value if you need to cause all sorts of aggravations to you and your surroundings to gather and accumulate it if you're not even going to be able to bring it with you when you pass away?

If this one-thousand dollars is the only way you can ensure your survival, buy food and pay the rent, then maybe you can be a little more determined in getting it back. However, you can do what you have to do to and still do your best to remain happy in the process. In this case, we're not speaking of drama but of survival. But look yourself straight in the eyes and ask: is this truly a matter of survival? Or is it rather pride?

If it doesn't really change a thing on the course of events, if your survival is not threatened, then it's pride. What happens if you let go? Karma will take care of it. You will be freed of a thousand dollars worth of karma that you stole before, which you just happen not to remember (or maybe you do) Never think that you've been the poster boy for virtue all your life... maybe that "lost" thousand dollars is karma that you're paying back.

Or, you can go a step further in remaining happy, and declare that it was never a thousand dollars. it was never even money, and it certainly wasn t yours. Before, it was a means to an end, such as going to the movies, and now, by letting go of it, it allows you to express compassion by training you to become more powerful, more happy and more immovable than your little insecure, squirmish-prone egotistic human self. In fact, it would be a perfect setup to use as a stepping stone to conquer drama. Like bodybuilders and strongmen use their muscles by putting them under greater and greater loads, that one-thousand dollars is a nice "load" to dissolve the belief that it even exists.

Just as there is no courage without fear, you cannot master yourself without actually facing drama head on. You cannot conquer drama without that moron who does believe in it and who has decided that he won't give you back your money. You're still alive. You can still be happy. You can move on. It is through situations like these that not only do you have great opportunities to conquer drama and become better at it in the process, but you also dissolve karma which you may have accumulated in the past without even realizing it or "gaining" good karma for the future.

You can use those kind of situations to train yourself at becoming a better human. By better human, please don't get caught up in the usual meaning of the labels. Like I said many times before, there's no better, and there's no human. I'm not speaking about that at all, but I need to use the words that are available to me in order for me to try to refer to some experiences that you have. You're not better, nor worse, and you're not human, you're a soul, a Self. Try to refine your understanding of what "becoming a better human" really means. A being at peace with being devoid of identity, of belongings, of relationships. This is what I mean. A free and very happy being indeed.

Remember what I said about death? No identity, no relationships, no properties. This is what death teaches us. Resolve those issues before death comes along and forces it upon you, so that when it comes it is a wonderful spiritual experience, which you won't fear nor be stressed about. You will just leave your body in peace and painlessly, and maybe even at the time of your own chosing, in a great state of happiness, conscious that all things are impermanent.

Integration doesn't need to be done only when you experience suffering. If something outside of you actually makes you react with joy, you can also integrate it, until you get to the state of Buddhahood where there's absolutely no way to find out if you are a Buddha, but you just know you are. At that point, you never will manifest a way to validate your "level", because you won't care about comparing yourself with anything and you'll be free of any type of attachment anyway.

For example, you may feel like copulating, and you can't or you're not allowed. Enjoy the abscence of satisfaction. Discover it by observing it consciously instead of only reacting. Observe the suffering until it disappears. You will become more and more conscious now that your body doesn't have power over you anymore, and you're not suffering anymore from the lack of sexual satisfaction. You won't care.

This is yet another occasion to create drama out of nowhere. You blame the spouse that they are not satisfying you. Well, whatever you seek outside, seek it inside, and I'm not speaking about self-gratification, although you are allowed to. I'm talking about what you are trying to find through sexual intercourse that you could instead exist as in a state of being inside your soul to satisfy. When you want an orgasm, you do not want to be happy, you simply want to stop suffering from the abscence of orgasm.

I understand now that as a teenager, I didn't want to be happy, I only wanted to relieve myself from the pressure of this sexual tension. Sexuality sought outside is simply hoping to stop suffering, it's not wanting to be happy. We are biologically built to do that, so do it, and enjoy it! Be responsible about your sexuality, and have fun! Just don't let it have power over you. Just do not allow it to put you in a state of unhappiness when it is not happening. Do not allow it to become a drama that you believe in. When abscence of sexuality is sufficient to put you in a state of unease, look at the suffering until it dissolves, and let go of the expectations.

Stop telling yourself: "Well it's normal to want to have an orgasm!" Yes it is. And as I've mentionned often: it's also normal to suffer. You can stop being normal. Does it mean that you'll be deprived of the ability to have sexuality? Not at all. It simply means that you'll be able to enjoy it when you have it, and you'll be able to enjoy life when you don't have it. I'm not free from the ability to have sex, but I'm free of the power it has to make me unhappy.

Do you sometimes feel afraid that you're not existing? Everybody has this place inside afraid that we may not exist. This is the ego that knows it's identity is a fraud, and it wants to avoid you finding out. Dwell into it! Dive into it! Enjoy it! You may feel like crap afraid that you don't exist! This is a wonderful place to be: it's the first step towards true freedom! Go into the emotion, this is a cause of suffering and depression.

I'm trying to release your state of mind about how much work there is to do to get there. Many people think that it's a lot of work. Having this mindset is entertaining drama yet again. I have students sometimes who, after a few months of having started an intense integration process, they begin to think that they still have so much more to do... It's a misconception. Don't think that there is a lot of work left before you're done. This process is ongoing, you're never going to be done. Eventually though, it will stop being painful, it might even become comfortable, or even fun! You'll like finding out about your patterns. I love looking at my ego! When I do and stumble upon an impression of separation, I think to myself: "Oh! I just saw an animal behavior there! Great, let me dissolve it."

It's not a goal to reach. Only the ego wants to reach goals. Those who want to reach enlightenment set themselves up in the best way possible to never actually enlighten at all. You don't reach englightenment.

And by the way, by now, you should understand that the very title of this book is an impossibility. You cannot conquer drama. Again, it is the ego who wants to conquer, to defeat, to win. Your Self doesn't care about all this- at all.

You can only be happy, free of the concept of having conquered anything.

www.ingramcontent.com/pod-product-compliance
Lightning Source LLC
Chambersburg PA
CBHW061432040426
42450CB00007B/1021